This book is dedicated to the leaders in our schools—teachers and principals alike—who do this important work every day.

INSIGHTS INTO
Action

SUCCESSFUL SCHOOL LEADERS
SHARE WHAT WORKS

WILLIAM **STERRETT**

Alexandria, Virginia USA

1703 N. Beauregard St. • Alexandria, VA 22311-1714 USA
Phone: 800-933-2723 or 703-578-9600 • Fax: 703-575-5400
Website: www.ascd.org • E-mail: member@ascd.org
Author guidelines: www.ascd.org/write

Gene R. Carter, *Executive Director;* Judy Zimny, *Chief Program Development Officer;* Gayle Owens, *Managing Director, Content Acquisitions and Development;* Scott Willis, *Director, Book Acquisitions & Development;* Laura Lawson, *Acquisitions Editor;* Julie Houtz, *Director, Book Editing & Production;* Miriam Goldstein, *Editor;* Sima Nasr, *Senior Graphic Designer;* Mike Kalyan, *Production Manager;* BMWW, *Typesetter;* Sarah Plumb, *Production Specialist.*

All web links in this book are correct as of the publication date below but may have become inactive or otherwise modified since that time. If you notice a deactivated or changed link, please e-mail books@ascd.org with the words "Link Update" in the subject line. In your message, please specify the web link, the book title, and the page number on which the link appears.

Unless otherwise cited, all quoted material is derived from interviews by the author and published with permission from the interviewees.

ASCD Member Book, No. FY12-3 (Dec. 2011, P). ASCD Member Books mail to Premium (P), Select (S), and Institutional Plus (I+) members on this schedule: Jan., PSI+; Feb., P; Apr., PSI+; May, P; July, PSI+; Aug., P; Sept., PSI+; Nov., PSI+; Dec., P. Select membership was formerly known as Comprehensive membership.

PAPERBACK ISBN: 978-1-4166-1368-8   ASCD product #112009
Also available as an e-book (see Books in Print for the ISBNs).

Quantity discounts for the paperback edition only: 10–49 copies, 10%; 50+ copies, 15%; for 1,000 or more copies, call 800-933-2723, ext. 5634, or 703-575-5634. For desk copies: member@ascd.org.

Library of Congress Cataloging-in-Publication Data

Sterrett, William.
    Insights into action : successful school leaders share what works / William Sterrett.
        p. cm.
    Includes bibliographical references and index.
    ISBN 978-1-4166-1368-8 (pbk. : alk. paper)
    1. Educational leadership.   2. School management and organization.   3. School improvement programs.   I. Title.
    LB2805.S7457 2011
    371.2—dc23

                                                            2011034270

22 21 20 19 18 17 16 15 14 13 12 11   1 2 3 4 5 6 7 8 9 10 11 12

INSIGHTS INTO *Action*

Section 1: Learning to Lead

Section 2: Strengthening the Learning Community

Section 3: Challenges for Today

Acknowledgments

I would like to thank, with great respect and appreciation, the following people.

First and foremost, I would like to thank my family: my wife, Stephanie, and our three boys, Will, Jack, and Graham, for their love and patience with me through my work. I am grateful for my parents, Clay and Teresa, who supported me in this effort as they have throughout my life, and my brother, Dave, who is himself a reflective author and gave me perspective in the early forming of my proposal. I want to thank my in-laws (how many authors can do that?) as well: Steve and Carol, thanks for your support of our family while I have taken extra time and energy to produce this work.

I would also like to thank the people in the schools whom I have worked with and who have given me insights, energy, and confidence in my work. I want to thank those in Jessamine County Schools in Kentucky for their support of me as I began my work as a middle school science teacher. I want to thank the folks in Charlottesville City Schools in Virginia for helping to develop me further as a teacher and a leader. I am grateful to those at Albemarle County Public Schools for their support of a novice principal and the continuation of that support throughout my tenure at a wonderful elementary school. And this work would not have been possible without great support throughout the University of North Carolina at Wilmington as I made the transition from principal to professor.

You cannot lead without having learned. In becoming an educator, I was profoundly influenced by a number of inspiring, encouraging faculty and staff members at Asbury University, Kentucky, who encouraged me to think critically. Likewise, as I completed my graduate degrees at the University of Virginia, I learned much about the importance of theory, practice, and reflection, which has helped shape this work.

Two professional organizations have helped me find my voice. I want to thank the Virginia branch of ASCD (VASCD) for giving me the opportunity to publish and present early in my educational leadership career. I also want to thank the Milken Family Foundation for striving to recognize and connect educators throughout the United States in a powerful, meaningful, and collaborative way.

This is my first book, and I am greatly indebted to the staff at ASCD for their diligence, patience, and support throughout this process. My developmental editor, Laura Lawson, provided helpful feedback and insights, and I am very grateful. Miriam Goldstein similarly helped me wordsmith my manuscript into a book that would have meaning in the hands of principals and teachers.

Finally, this work would not have been possible without the educators who contributed so much to the book. Jane Foley, I am indebted to you for your early advice and for writing such a meaningful foreword. This book has been strengthened incredibly by the powerful and thoughtful voices of educators who have "been there, done that" in so many ways, including Baruti Kafele, Rick DuFour, Alex Carter, Carol Ann Tomlinson, Temple Grandin, Roxann Kriete, Richard Louv, Pam Moran, Ira Socol, James Popham, and Yvonne Chan. May your voices as leaders and as learners influence many more in the days and years ahead.

Foreword

> Leadership and learning are indispensable to each other.
>
> —*John F. Kennedy*

With *Insights into Action,* author William Sterrett invites us to learn, to think, and, as an added bonus, to apply as we lead. Sounds like good medicine indeed for the overwhelmed, overworked, and, yes, sometimes confused leaders in the field.

In my role as leader of the Milken Educator Awards initiative at the Milken Family Foundation (www.mff.org), I have the honor and distinct pleasure of traveling around the country. After visiting hundreds of our nation's top-performing schools in urban, suburban, and rural settings, and meeting and learning from thousands of successful educators, I was excited to learn of William's project to talk with successful educators, capture their unique and compelling stories, and share them with other educators.

As an educational leader, you are faced with a literal mountain of reading: memos, monthly periodicals or briefings, e-mails, blogs, web links, education reports, news articles, and more. So why is this book different? Why should it be the next educational book you will actually read cover to cover, and don't relegate to your usual skim of titles, subheads, and bullet points, or, worse yet, place in your black-hole reading pile to address "at some point"?

Why? Because *Insights into Action* is equal parts information, wisdom, and inspiration. It provides case studies of individuals selected because they are exemplars who have received numerous external recognitions for their individual contributions as well as acknowledgment for their roles in transforming organizations and the education system itself.

The stories in the following nine chapters not only blend the best of theory and practice; every chapter also comes with its own leadership "lesson plans"—a series of practical reflective questions and In-the-Field Activities.

High school principal Baruti Kafele in Newark, New Jersey, shares his laserlike focus on changing the attitudes of students, which will in turn change their achievement. In fact, after only five years, his high school, with an 85 percent poverty rate, registered a 95 percent graduation rate. If you think that isn't possible in your school, consider his actions.

Rick DuFour, the national voice of professional learning communities, shares that he had only three all-faculty meetings a year when he was a high school principal. How is that possible in a school that helped launch the successful PLC national movement? His insights led to the development of actions that transformed the way teachers and schools collaborate.

Is professional growth plus personal balance even possible for the 24/7 life of an educational leader? Young high school principal Alex Carter, in the high-achieving and equally high-pressure community of Telluride, Colorado, provides straightforward actions for you that are *almost* as easy as 1, 2, 3.

For years, renowned educator and author Carol Ann Tomlinson has been articulating the rationale and strategies that prepare teachers to use differentiated instruction with their students. Chapter 4 takes us to the next level and addresses the parallel importance for leaders to incorporate differentiated approaches when working with individual teachers and building the organization as a whole.

Drawing on the work of author and former teacher Roxann Kriete, Chapter 5 provides commonsense tools for teachers and school leaders to transform a school culture from one consumed with and reacting to discipline issues to one that successfully focuses on common goals and maximizing learning opportunities. The foundation of such a culture springs from strong leadership that fosters relationship building within classrooms and throughout the school environment.

In Chapter 6, we learn from Richard Louv, author and advocate of environment-based education, the why and the how of incorporating learning experiences outside—literally—the classroom. School leaders can educate and motivate staff to engage students by creating a partnership of nature and learning, and thereby improve behavior, health, and achievement in core academic areas.

A division superintendent and one of *eSchoolNews*'s Top 10 Tech-Savvy Superintendents of 2010, Pam Moran makes the infusion of technology into every facet of her division an urgent priority for students, staff, and the community. She models use of technology, provides universal access to information and the latest technologies, develops shared ownership, and consistently aligns instruction with the needs of students in a 21st century world.

Assessment expert James Popham helps us examine the power of formative assessment by asking and acting on two essential questions: "Is an adjustment needed, and, if so, what should that adjustment be?" Chapter 8 helps leaders structure a yearlong framework to create authentic ongoing assessments that emphasize shared planning, quick checks for understanding, proactive adjustments, and, most important, assessments that function as an instructional tool.

We would be remiss to ignore the elephant in the room: the daily, monthly, yearly, lifelong challenges at the micro and macro levels. It is appropriate that we look to charter-school pioneer Yvonne Chan from Los Angeles, California, and her insights on overcoming challenges. Yvonne has weathered many educational storms, and after 42 years in education, she is still known for her educational innovation, dynamic and motivational presentations, and, above all, her ability to lift everyone around her and inspire others to act.

You are reading this foreword out of your commitment to lifelong learning. Johann Wolfgang Von Goethe said, "A great person attracts great people and knows how to hold them together." You can be that great person. *Insights into Action* offers both practical lessons and inspiration to face the challenges ahead. Now you are ready for action, too.

Jane Foley, Ph.D.
Senior Vice President, Milken Educator Awards, Milken Family Foundation
1994 Indiana Milken Educator

Introduction

At some point during my first year as an elementary school principal, I looked out of my office window at the winter landscape and thought, "Am I really prepared for this?" I was 28 years old, did not have an assistant principal, and was facing the prospect of telling my staff that one of our colleagues had just passed away. Earlier in the week, an angry parent had informed me that she was "contacting a lawyer," and I had several discipline referrals sitting on top of the stacks of paper that covered my desk. I turned from the window and saw my phone's red message light flashing. I was lucky enough to be working with some trusted veteran administrators in the district who had taken me under their wing, and I knew I could count on them for advice, wisdom, and a chance to simply share my difficulties and challenges with them. And yet, at that moment, I felt very alone.

In my first year as a principal, I faced enormous challenges. By all accounts, I was ready for the job. I had a solid track record of teaching, had served as an assistant principal, and held a Ph.D. in educational administration and supervision. My school division was rich in resources, and I had attended a host of useful conferences and professional development sessions. But I just could not escape that feeling of frantically bustling about like a race-car pit crew near the end of a tight race.

A Need for Insight

I realized early on that in a job filled with constant stressors and challenges, it was important for me to have a solid, well-grounded perspective that I continually renewed by soaking in relevant research in the field. But I struggled to find literature that incorporated a healthy marriage of effective action research and current theoretical understandings.

Combing educational journals and catalogs for the latest works on school leadership, I struggled to connect the writings and conference presentations with the specific challenges that I faced day to day. At times, the work was relevant and led to actual change in my building. Other times, even the best-selling books seemed dry or irrelevant, lacking that important in-the-field component. I wondered, "Do they really get it? Do they really know my reality of facing the teacher who is fed up with her negative colleague? Do they really know what it's like to observe a teacher doing everything she can and yet still know that her student, who just transferred to our school three grade levels behind in reading, is not going to pass the high-stakes assessment? Does that author know what it's like, as a Title I principal, to constantly worry about having a "failing school" label pinned to his school? Does that presenter know what it's like to see students trail in Monday morning from the bus hungry and upset because they have hardly eaten the entire weekend?"

Lessons from the Field

The educators who I always knew "got it" have been those with engaging voices in the field. My colleagues, too, would perk up when a principal stood to share an approach that had led to sustained success in his or her building. Similarly, we would lean in to hear a science teacher talk about differentiating instruction to 26 students in a mixed-level class because we knew she was reporting to work the next day and *living* a narrative of teaching and learning.

Despite facing many challenges as a principal, I was also fortunate to see incredible successes. Our school received recognitions such as the Distinguished Title I School Award and the Governor's Board of Education Excellence award. And I was shocked and humbled to receive a Milken National Educator award in a surprise afternoon assembly in our school gymnasium. This life-changing experience led me to meet a host of other practitioners across the United States who shared their insights and success narratives. I got to meet educators who had beaten the odds and turned around failing districts faced with economic and social challenges, and talented teachers who reached diverse students with engaging lessons.

And they were willing to share. Listening to their words and hearing the names of their students brought a renewed perspective to me. Hearing a colleague describe how he had organized a framework for collaboration and shared leadership to cut back on meetings and maximize ownership gave me hope. Seeing a fellow principal walk through classrooms and ask students to describe, in their own words, what they were learning motivated me to do the same in my school. Hearing about "Anthony" making nearly a year's worth of growth in just six months, "Nathaniel" thriving in school after losing both parents to legal difficulties, and "Renalda," who had declared that she *hated* reading, having a determined teacher "light her fire" and foster a love for learning and discovery, sparked my own desire to share their stories.

Insights into Action

These powerful insights also brought to life many of the readings that were dry or lacking in relevance. So, as a new professor of educational leadership, I vowed that my work would address those questions that I had so long sought to answer.

I do not even pretend to have all the answers, so fortunately, this book is not just about me. Instead, I merge current research and theory with practical lessons from nine talented and successful educators in the field who have truly "been there, done that" in their roles as principals, team or department heads, or teacher leaders. As a former teacher and administrator, I had the opportunity to lead and to learn. In this book, I have paused to reflect and to draw on my own experiences, as well as on the insights of others. I am humbled by the company I keep in these chapters.

Practical Lessons for School Leaders

This book focuses on relevant topics that face today's educational leaders, particularly those at the school level: teacher leaders, grade or department chairs, assistant principals, and principals. Each chapter weaves a narrative of a successful leader who embodies the characteristics that current research and theory have established as essential for success. Each chapter examines a different topic and offers practical applications and ways to overcome barriers to success. In addition, every chapter includes Action Items and In-the-Field Activities to help readers realize actual change and growth in their schools.

We face many challenges in our daily roles as educators and leaders. This work can be hard and, at times, cause us to question ourselves. But there are answers out there, and many of them are not as far off as we might imagine. We all have much to learn; in the chapters ahead, may we learn together.

Section 1

Learning to Lead

1

Turning Vision into Reality

The number-one determinant of a school's success is the leader. I have to be throughout the school. When people are on the school grounds, they have got to see and feel my leadership in the lobby, to feel me, throughout the halls.

—Baruti Kafele

Action Items
* Make morning announcements
* Send a daily e-mail to staff
* Attend community events
* Conduct effective meetings

A Living Vision

"Good morning, good morning, good morning," the booming voice intones as students step off the bus and onto the school grounds. Principal Baruti Kafele extends his hand to and makes eye contact with every student as he or she enters the building—*his* building. Minutes later, over the public announcement system, he urges students to "have your best day yet while maintaining a positive attitude." Not content to sit behind his desk and push papers, Kafele stresses the importance of articulating a vision and then modeling that vision each day—during each classroom visit, each conversation with a staff member, and each discussion with a parent.

Principal Kafele embodies what researchers call *change leadership*. He began his career in education as a substitute teacher in Brooklyn. Just completing his fourth principalship, Kafele is known for taking the reins of a school in crisis and transforming the entire school community. He served for the last five years at Newark Tech High School in Newark, New Jersey, a school where more than 85 percent of students are eligible for free or reduced-price lunch—and one that boasts a graduation rate of over 95 percent. Named a 2009 Milken National Educator, Kafele is author of the best-selling book *Motivating Black Males to Achieve in School and in Life* and speaks to audiences across the United States. He credits his schools' successes to his *vision* and his *visibility*.

The Importance of Vision

In interviewing Principal Kafele, I quickly realized that he believes the school leader is *the* essential component in realizing a meaningful vision. He is not shy about noting the critical factor to transformative change in an education system: "It's me," he says bluntly. "I don't care what the circumstances of the students are—where they are from, their home life. We have to see success in them, we have to envision excellence in them. That drives everything I say, everything I think, everything I do as a leader. . . . The number-one determinant of a school's success is the leader."

Researcher Judith Kafka (2009) agrees, noting that "a growing body of literature suggests that there is a discernible relationship between school leaders' actions and student achievement" (p. 318). Goldring and Schuermann (2009) take it further, asserting that "today's educational leaders need to motivate community-mindedness to address communitywide problems that are central to schools and the current imperatives of student achievement" (p. 16).

Kafele stresses, however, that school success cannot rest on one leader's personality. As he explains, "My focus is having the students develop a vision for themselves and transforming their attitudes, taking ownership of the vision. The rest—the test scores and achievement gaps—will take care of themselves."

Forming, articulating, and living such a vision is crucial to sustained leadership in a school. Schools and other organizations spend an abundance of time on developing their visions, often bringing in outside consultants to help. A school's vision should be more than empty words plastered on a marquee sign; it must have rich, relevant meaning. It is up to the leader to embody this vision every day. Each and every interaction serves as an opportunity to highlight where the school is headed.

When I became an elementary school principal in 2006, I wrote a letter to the community introducing myself and inviting parents to come in over the summer months to meet and chat. Little did I know how busy those "slow" summer months would be. Questions abounded about "the new guy," and I'll never forget the first parent who came into my office. I tried to make small talk and ask about her summer, but she got right to the point. "Dr. Sterrett," she said, looking me straight in the eyes, "what is your vision for the school?" I paused. I recognized the importance of the question and knew that the answer wasn't something I could just whip up or pull from a book. My response had to be sincere and relevant, and it had to speak to her child's success. My mind raced, and I searched for something profound to say. Eventually, I came up with "challenging all students to achieve high levels of success," which was apparently acceptable to the parent, who respectfully nodded in agreement. But that question stuck with me for years.

Visions drive organizations into the future. Bolman and Deal (2003) note that "*vision* turns an organization's core ideology, or sense of purpose, into an image of what the future might become" (p. 252). Because of the importance of vision to a school, it must be clear to the entire school community. Sparks (2007) observes that successful leaders must "cultivate clarity regarding values and fundamental purposes that are most important" (p. 13).

In today's schools, particularly in high schools such as the one that Kafele leads, educators value their creativity and autonomy. Some independently minded educators may equate articulating a consistent, clear vision with attempting to herd cats. Fortunately, autonomy and shared vision are not mutually exclusive. Kafele maintains that staff members can coexist and thrive under a common vision. He secures the support of his staff by rejecting micromanagement in favor of tying teachers' individual strengths to a shared vision of success for all students.

Kafele believes in keeping vision statements simple. Use one sentence—two at most—and make sure it identifies a clear direction. Kafele's most recent school's vision statement is "Newark Tech will become a national model of urban educational excellence" (Essex County Vocational Technical Schools, 2011). This simple, concise statement is easily memorized and understood. And, as demonstrated by the many awards and accolades received by the school, it has been achieved.

The Importance of Visibility

Vision and visibility are necessarily intertwined for today's school leaders. Whereas each is important in its own right, given the numerous challenges that today's building leader faces, they must be fused together to sustain success.

Principal Kafele's tall frame is often seen striding down the hallways of his school, from room to room, with the deliberate purpose of interacting with students. He explains, "You show me a school with a principal behind the desk, and I'll show you a school without principal leadership." The successful principal must be constantly "taking the pulse" of the school community. Kafele views successful visibility through both an individual and a team lens, noting that "in basketball, you recall Larry Bird and Magic Johnson were often out there and visible, though they were also content to allow the team around them to grow and win. Sometimes they carried the team, other times they were more in the periphery, but together they won." Similarly, Kafele notes that although he is usually "out there" serving as a visible leader, he can't be everywhere at once; to realize sustained success, he must have a strong team around him.

Above all, Kafele stresses availability and consistency as the key elements of visibility.

Availability

Kafele ensures that he is constantly available to those with whom he works, particularly students. In a video documentary about Principal Kafele (Milken Family Foundation, 2010), a parent happily observes that "his students have his cell phone number; they can call him 24 hours [a day], and that's really unheard of." He has also been known to tweet news of students' achievements from airports while awaiting connecting flights.

Other educators may make themselves available through designated online office hours during which they respond immediately to e-mails or instant messages about school-related issues. Availability might mean attending a community breakfast at a local housing complex to celebrate a tutoring program in the district, or it might mean dropping by a Little League game where a number of students and families congregate. Availability says, "I am working with you—here, in our community—to make a difference. You matter to me, and I want our work to matter to you." Although the means of availability may differ, the importance of it does not.

Consistency

Successful educational leaders build regular "touch points" into their day during which they consistently reach out to the school community. Kafele's touch points occur during students' arrival at the beginning of the day, morning announcements, and daily classroom visits. Other principals may make sure to attend certain sporting events or engage in community activities. However leaders choose to structure their touch points, they must be willing to be a visible presence, even at the end of a grueling day. Members of the school community appreciate being able to count on seeing their leaders consistently. As the new principal of a school that had recently experienced rapid turnover of principals, I realized that establishing routines and consistently following them built important relational trust. I asked our music teacher to identify and update a school song, which provided us with a new Friday morning ritual of song and celebration over the intercom. I served as a Bingo caller for the community night picnic. And I swallowed my pride each year and participated in the annual talent show, usually with a break-dancing routine. These touch-point opportunities were a way for me to be a lead player in the school community, and students, staff, and parents soon looked to me (and my colleagues) to lead and share. This consistent involvement fed an expectation of sharing my vision for greater school community in a visible, tangible way. If a school's vision includes "growing together as a community," then the school leader must be an active presence and willing to build trust, share laughs, and interact in a meaningful way.

24-Hour Visibility

The role of educational leader can be compared to the fast-paced 24-hour news cycle. Educators, like politicians or other headliners, cannot escape public scrutiny—even in the grocery store! As a principal, I was keenly aware of what was in my grocery cart when I shopped after a long workday. Parents and students would come up to me, often just to say hello—but maybe to peek in my cart, too! It comes with the territory. Although we might not feel comfortable giving out our cell phone numbers to the school community, we should always be mindful that we are public servants and find ways to use our "celebrity" to promote our vision. When you encounter students and their parents at the carnival or the local park, remind them of the next school event or praise the students' recent achievement gains. When we live the life of a visible leader, reinforcing the vision should come naturally.

Overcoming Challenges

Putting forth a vision and then living it is no small task. In a school setting, the principal is the leader in articulating and living the vision. However, he or she cannot, and must not, do this work alone. Shared leadership is vitally important here. As Johnson (2008) puts it, "A principal with vision and expertise creates a blueprint of how the school can achieve its goals. He or she finds teachers and staff to help make that vision a reality. The principal continually coaches and mentors the staff so that together they can accomplish the desired results" (p. 72).

Many leaders can quickly be derailed or lose the support of their school communities by failing to recognize what the organization is doing right and affirming "quick wins" that are already occurring, or by simply not getting the job done. The leader must be a doer and bring the organization—the department or school—along in realizing the vision.

Work from the Current State

A successful school leader understands the current state—the reality as it stands *now*. Recognizing the current state requires both personal reflection and the ability to manage and make decisions based on data. As Patterson and colleagues (2008) note in the book *Influencer*, it is important to "diagnose before you prescribe" (p. 258). This multifaceted understanding enables the leader to foster change and growth in the organization. A successful leader will be able and willing to adapt the school's vision to the ever-changing current state to facilitate continued success.

Find "Quick Wins"

It is important that the leader notch some quick wins to demonstrate that success is not only possible, but is also happening now. Doug Reeves (2009) advises leaders to "pull the weeds before you plant the flowers" (p. 13)—that is, reduce existing and less essential initiatives to clear space for the critical items that they are "drowning under" (p. 14). Establishing clear priorities creates a sense of authenticity and demonstrates that the leader will do what it takes to support the common vision. Many successful principals make seemingly minor improvements, such as adding a coat of paint or mulching the grounds to rejuvenate the school's immediate appearance. These actions will build momentum and align support for a shared, larger vision that encompasses every aspect of the school community.

Follow Through

As obvious as it sounds, it is nonetheless essential for the leader to ensure that the work aligned with the vision gets done. As the saying goes, "Leadership is about action, not position." Simply manning the desk in an efficient manner does not make a great principal; rather, greatness lies in the transformative steps that the leader takes each day to make the vision come alive. Bossidy and Charan (2002) note that although planning and envisioning are important, it is *execution* that is the key role of the leader. Educational leaders will be seen as truly transformative when actual, noticeable change is occurring—particularly when that change is aligned with the vision that has been shared and lived in a consistent, visible manner. Davies and Brighouse (2010) note that "values without implementation do little for the school. It is in the tackling of difficult challenges to change and improve, often by confronting unacceptable practices, that passionate leaders show their educational values" (p. 4).

Baruti Kafele notes that plenty of his peer principals have identified the same challenges that he has and are just as aware of best practices and necessary next steps. Not all leaders, however, are successful at effective implementation through a determined, visionary approach. When Kafele was an assistant principal, "One of the first things I did was get permission from my principal to change the look of the building by putting up motivational messages and images and speak on the PA system to have morning announcements. I needed to change the climate and culture. The very next year, I was principal of the school."

A few specific action items can make a significant difference in realizing a school's vision.

Action Items

Without action, a vision is just a piece of paper. In education, we have lots of paper; sometimes, it doesn't mean much at all. For the vision to be achieved, it must be seen as something vibrant and real. The following Action Items will help ensure that your school's vision thrives.

Make Morning Announcements

Kafele says, "One thing that makes me cringe is when I am visiting a school and the day starts and the bell rings, and I don't hear the principal's voice over the intercom first thing. [Students] have got to see me first thing; they have got to hear me. It begins with morning announcements. Those interactions, conversations, and delivering that motivational message each morning to reverberate throughout the building" convey a message of high expectations to students. Kafele structures his announcements to include these four components:

- A greeting;
- An inspirational thought;
- Highlights of success within the school; and
- A challenge to begin the day.

Kafele's announcements are a consistent, visible way to communicate his school's vision, and the school community has come to rely on hearing his voice each morning. His superintendent notes that he is a "master teacher" through his use of morning announcements to recognize student success and, when necessary, encourage students to complete work, meet deadlines, and achieve to their capabilities.

Send a Daily E-mail to Staff

In a world where teachers and staff are inundated with communications, administrative e-mails are often met with groans and cringes—if the messages get noticed at all. I resolved this problem in my own school by starting to send a concise daily e-mail (see Figure 1.1 for an example) that contained

Figure 1.1 | **Principal Daily E-mail**

Good morning, staff. Here are a few items for today, Monday, February 1st.

1. There will be a **Fire Drill** at 8:25 a.m. Please review expectations with your students prior to this and remember that it is below freezing this morning!

2. **Team PLC Meetings**

   a. 1st Grade—8:45 in Ms. Smith's room

   b. 4th Grade—11:45 in Ms. Jones's room

3. **Faculty Meeting this Thursday**. Please bring your writing sample and rubric guide. Refreshments by the 2nd grade team.

4. Upcoming—**Schoolwide Field Trips** to Cape Caverns next week

   a. Tuesday (Feb. 9)—K–2 teams depart at 8 a.m. and return at 2 p.m.

   b. Wednesday (Feb. 10)—3rd–5th grade teams depart at 8 a.m. and return at 2 p.m.

5. **Quote** for the day: Learning is a treasure that will follow its owner everywhere. (Chinese proverb)

Have a great day!

Dr. Sterrett

---

useful information and administrative minutiae while also tying in the overarching vision of the organization (Sterrett, 2008). Consistently providing a single point of communication, affirmation, and clarification to start each day shows staff members that you view their "think time" as a valuable resource.

Attend Community Events

A school's vision is not confined within the walls of the school building or to the hours of the school day. Today's educational leader must be prepared to be an active, visible embodiment of the work of the school throughout the community and even through such venues as the evening news, Twitter, and YouTube. Baruti Kafele speaks to audiences of students and staff throughout the United States, and he ensures that his message is consistent and visible by using modern technologies and by staying on message about what's important: realizing student success. Speaking engagements and meetings—opportunities many educational leaders have—are great forums for leaders to reiterate vision. In addition, community events provide opportunities to engage the school community and live the vision. For example, a high school principal might make a deliberate attempt to shake students' hands at a basketball game and ask them about their Spanish club work. An elementary assistant principal might dress up as Dr. Seuss for the Wednesday reading night. And the enthusiastic teacher who dons the mascot outfit at the restaurant fundraiser will not be forgotten!

Conduct Effective Meetings

School leaders should be wary of meetings. In his book *Death by Meeting,* Patrick Lencioni (2004) refers to them as the "most painful problem in business" and poses the question, "How pathetic is it that we have come to accept that the activity most central to the running of our organizations is inherently painful and unproductive?" (p. viii). Educational leaders have the power to change meetings for the better, however. Kafele holds only one staff meeting each month. He says, "I have very little time to have meetings, and when I do, I want the staff to know that they are important and that I have a clear message that is tied to my vision." Author Rick DuFour notes that, as a principal, he held only three full faculty meetings each year!

Meetings are valuable for communicating important information, but they must be interactive. As a principal, I realized that most of what I needed to communicate in terms of "one-way" updates (or even—gasp!—directives) could be done via e-mail. In my fourth year as principal, I structured meetings solely to affirm staff, share highlights from within, and give teachers the opportunity to work together (see Figure 1.2 for a sample meeting format).

We opened our meetings by bestowing the "Woody Bear award" on a staff member. This oversized, stuffed teddy bear in a school-spirit polo shirt was a token of appreciation passed from one staff member to another. Each meeting would start with the current guardian of Woody Bear reading a short announcement of affirmation and giving Woody Bear to a colleague. We cheered loudly, announced the honoree on the intercom, and placed the news on our school web page. Affirmation can be all too rare, but Woody Bear ensured that it was a regular part of our routine.

Education can be an isolating field, and we tend not to see the work of our colleagues regularly. So we used a portion of our weekly faculty meeting to share a classroom highlight, either by video clip or through a demonstration. Teachers got great ideas from one another and gained insights on how

Figure 1.2 | Monthly Meeting Format Example

What	Who	Duration (approximate)
Refreshments and conversation	Teams (or departments) rotate each month	First 10 minutes
Opening agenda (purpose of the meeting)	Principal	2 minutes
Recognitions: "Woody Bear award" to a staff member; example highlight clips of teaching, testimonial	Principal, teachers	8 minutes
Introduction of stated instructional focus	Principal or teacher leader	5 minutes
Teamwork on the specific related focus area	Led by team (or dept.) teacher leader; all teachers participate	50 minutes
Wrap-up (optional), review of objectives, closing	Principal or team leader	5 minutes
	Total duration	1 hour 20 minutes

to engage students. This meeting segment provided an authentic opportunity for shared leadership and ownership of our collective work and displayed the great diversity of teaching approaches that led to student success.

Finally, having team time to work on instructional issues is essential. As a school leader, you can carve targeted, protected team time out of staff meetings. This time also provides an opportunity to interact with specific teams or have a division coordinator or colleague come and touch base with various teams.

The Importance of Reflection

The visible leader uses every opportunity to strengthen the vision among the learning community. This message is not constrained to meetings or to business cards; it is real, organic, and easily recognized. As leaders such as Baruti Kafele demonstrate, the role of educational leader is not for those unwilling to be a presence or to take some risks. By leading, the leader will stand on a pedestal—like it or not.

The effective visionary leader must constantly pause, however, to reflect on the vision. Be creative in finding opportunities for reflection. For example, if a student at Kafele's school makes a mistake, such as violating the dress code or using profanity, Kafele assigns them to a "read-a-thon," which entails staying after school and reading independently for one hour. Kafele not only monitors students but also participates, using the opportunity to read and reflect. "Where else do I get the time to read, uninterrupted, something that I actually want to read?" he asks. Constant visibility can be tiring, so finding time to reflect and recharge is essential. After all, if you aren't fully energized as you greet every student in the morning or grasp the PA microphone, you cannot sincerely convey a vision that is alive and evident to the entire school community. Beyond the noise and the energy of learning, we must remember to reflect, and to continue our *own* learning.

In-the-Field Activities

1. Select an educational leader (school, division, or nontraditional) and ask him or her to articulate the school's vision. Next, ask three stakeholders (student, parent, teacher, or another staff member) the same question. Are their answers aligned? Describe your findings and their implications.

2. Work with a school leader to create a faculty meeting format that incorporates the following items within a 90-minute time frame:
   a. Affirmation of the school community.
   b. Instructional highlights from within the building or department.
   c. Protected team time for instructional issues.

3. Review the Action Items from this chapter and develop a plan to implement at least one in your school setting. Consider Kafele's use of morning announcements, or my example of a daily e-mail, or the potential power of community events. What steps are needed, and how will you communicate them to your team? What challenges do you anticipate? How will you reflect on your work after implementation?

2

From School Leader to Learning Leader

Did the students really learn? How will we respond?

—Rick DuFour

Action Items
* Build a collaborative schedule
* Share a common format for minutes
* Involve staff in schoolwide progress reviews
* Conduct peer observations for leaders and teachers

A Learning Leader

As principals, our roles are numerous. At any given time, we may wear the hats of manager, event organizer, counselor, spokesperson, and analyst, among others. However, in this age of ever-increasing accountability, educational leaders are mandated to serve above all as *instructional leaders*. As Rick DuFour sees it, instructional leaders' essential task is to continually ask the question "Did the students really learn?" (personal communication, 2010). DuFour is a nationally known speaker, author of best-selling books about professional learning communities (PLCs), and former principal of Adlai Stevenson High School in Lincolnshire, Illinois. During his 10 years at Adlai Stevenson, DuFour and his school won numerous awards, including the Blue Ribbon School award.

Today's principals cannot manage a school on an efficiency model alone. Yes, school safety is paramount. Yes, the school must be clean, arrival and dismissal must run smoothly, events should promote the talents and energies of the school community, and teachers and students should feel that the school climate is conducive to growth. However, DuFour (2002) has offered a radical proposal in which he casts the principal as a "learning leader" who first and foremost promotes learning throughout the building.

Today's school leaders should embody these four principles:

1. **Believe That "Learning Is Fun."** As educational leaders, we must embrace and live by this mantra. We have a profound influence on our schools' culture and achievement, and we should model a love of learning and encourage all members of the school community to grow as lifelong learners.

2. **Be a Servant Leader.** School leaders should not be seen as above-the-fray icons but as active leaders who accomplish the real work of the school. Whether donning an apron to serve "trout treasures" when a cafeteria staff member has to leave to care for a sick child or delivering healthy snacks to students on a high-stakes testing day, it is the small, human touches that enable the leader to serve the school community in an authentic way.

3. **Apply External Leadership Principles.** DuFour believes that "principals and leaders should be voracious readers, particularly outside of education.

Read, for example, the *Harvard Business Review,* or leadership books that aren't necessarily education-related but in which the leader can learn something to apply to education."

4. **Insist on Relevance and Authenticity.** Instructional leaders must ensure that relevance and authenticity pervade the school's work. Meetings should be relevant. Work should be shared and jointly owned. A team approach should be genuine. And data should mean something.

PLCs and the Importance of Conversation

For DuFour's vision of instructional leadership to work, he says, "We need to create the conditions that allow the principal and teams of teachers to look at actual evidence of student achievement, and from that achievement look at what strategies are causing that data." Yet even successful leaders who have articulated a powerful vision and obtained buy-in can have trouble implementing a collaborative approach to instructional leadership. Enter DuFour's solution: professional learning communities. In an article for *Educational Leadership* titled "What Is a 'Professional Learning Community'?" DuFour (2004) notes that we should fundamentally "focus on learning rather than teaching, work collaboratively, and hold (ourselves) accountable for results" (p. 6). These PLCs are learning teams, usually formed as a department (such as a group of high school biology teachers) or grade-level team (such as a group of 3rd grade teachers) in which colleagues ask the critical questions that inform learning. Many schools and teams embrace the idea of PLCs, but I asked DuFour to share his principal's perspective in making sure that the teams work effectively.

Crucial Questions for PLC Collaboration

PLCs emphasize student learning, teacher collaboration, and results. DuFour notes "four crucial questions" that must guide the work of educators:

- What do we want each student to learn?
- How will we know when each student has learned it?
- How will we respond when a student experiences difficulty in learning?
- How will we respond when a student is proficient?

These four questions make sense. Yet answering these in a collaborative, authentic, and reflective manner is not always easy. As teachers grapple with the day-to-day demands of supervising, managing their classrooms, and differentiating instruction to meet students' needs, collaboration often gets pushed aside. Here's an example of what genuine PLC collaboration might look like:

A group of five teachers huddles around a kidney-shaped table in a 3rd grade classroom. The teachers hold sheets of paper filled with columns and rows labeled with student names and achievement data. They discuss the students and the results of specific assignments, in-class activities, and assessments. They speak with authentic engagement and passion. They give one another time to speak, and they listen. They hold up samples of student work. They point to the rows and then back to the student work. As the teachers discuss a student, they refer to the numbers—the various data—as real, meaningful. A teacher leans in to point at the curriculum map and discusses how she engaged students with three lessons on subtraction. Students who had previously struggled are now confident and making gains. Another teacher discusses two small-group strategies that she found helpful and describes how she set up her classroom to implement them. The teachers share and discuss student progress and data collaboratively and positively rather than blaming students or other conditions outside their control. It is clear from observing this team that its work is based on trust, which fosters genuine conversation—a conversation that will ultimately help students.

This fictitious scenario is very real in many successful schools. Five important factors, all embodied by the group in the scenario, enable professional learning communities to thrive:

- Trust.
- Honesty.
- A knowledge of students and their needs.
- Supportive, uncritical communication.
- A focus on learning for both students and staff.

Overcoming Challenges

DuFour believes that educational leaders show they are instructional leaders in a variety of ways, from how they approach meetings, to how they gather information, to how they overcome barriers. Here are some ways successful learning leaders deal with common challenges.

Manage Principal Time

A common barrier to supporting PLCs is school leaders' lack of time (or time management) and their resulting inability to monitor the PLCs' activity and progress in a consistent way. Principals must protect themselves from interruptions and purposefully schedule blocks of time to address e-mails and phone calls. "The idea of the open-door principalship is very appealing, the notion that people can come in at any time, but I don't think you can do that," DuFour cautions. "There are times where you need to close the door and focus on what impacts learning as opposed to responding to every little question that comes up along the way." You have to create structures, as DuFour notes, "beyond the principalship," because one person cannot do this work alone. As DuFour observes, "we have to let go of the mind-set that I can do it all myself."

Manage Schoolwide Time

According to DuFour, educational leaders have too long focused on items that are "high time and low leverage" instead of "low time and high leverage." He believes that all leaders should ask themselves, "What can I do that has the highest impact on student achievement?" He offers the following examples of high-leverage strategies:

- Have collaborative teams of teachers agree on the knowledge and skills that each student must acquire.
- Establish common pacing, outlining which topics should be taught in a given time frame.
- Gather evidence of student learning through a variety of assessments, including team-developed formative assessments.
- Use the assessment results to (1) provide struggling students with extra time and support through a systematic, schoolwide plan of timely intervention; (2) enrich and extend learning for students who are proficient; and (3) inform and improve professional practice.

Disperse Leadership

DuFour practices *dispersed leadership,* an approach that builds and makes use of leadership structures beyond the principalship. At Adlai Stevenson High School, he charged department chairs and team leaders with ensuring success on their teams. "That mind-set that I have to do it all has to go," he argues.

He also believes that principals should limit faculty meetings and instead focus on what matters: student achievement. "I had three full faculty meetings per year," he says. In place of those meetings, he met with department chairs for 30 minutes four days a week to go over managerial items (e.g., "How do I handle this parent phone call?") and held an additional two-hour weekly meeting with the chairs to focus solely on instructional leadership items. "My job as principal was to train the department chairs to lead their departments, not just to manage. The biggest part of their evaluations dealt with leadership and evidence of leadership. The department chairs then met with their team leaders—the math chair with the algebra chair, and so on."

What meetings there are should be useful and relevant. DuFour emphasizes the importance of role-play and rehearsal in leadership meetings in which superintendents work with principals or principals work with team leaders to address a concern or challenge together. Principal meetings, in which superintendents and principals work together, should mirror collaborative team meetings, and all present should be prepared "to be called upon to share evidence, share a concern, and ask for help together. . . . In any leadership position, we have crucial conversations, and meetings could provide an opportunity to role-play, get feedback, and discuss together how we can become more effective."

DuFour notes that "at my own school, I only met with team leaders four times a year, where we worked on professional growth items that *they* brought to the table. We were usually able to work on our growth by using the exemplars from within the building and rarely had to go outside." This cascading, layered approach to leadership (see Figure 2.1) allowed for shared ownership and built trust among his staff.

Keep in mind that even in a professional learning community, autonomy and trust should be prized. As an elementary school principal, I often asked

Figure 2.1 | A Cascading Pyramid Model of Dispersed Leadership

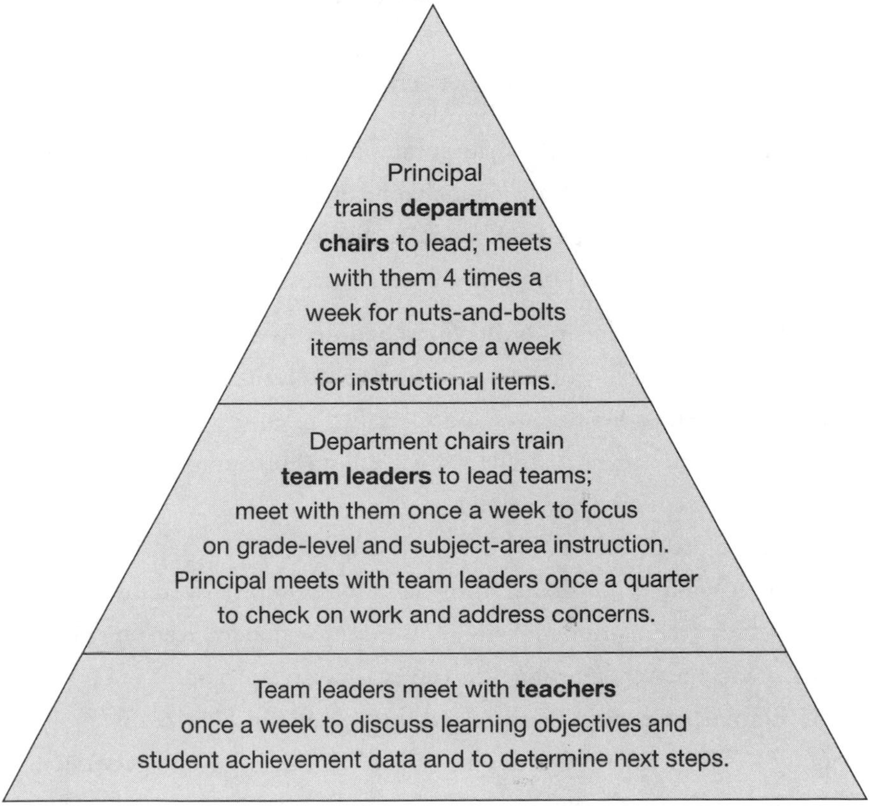

Principal trains **department chairs** to lead; meets with them 4 times a week for nuts-and-bolts items and once a week for instructional items.

Department chairs train **team leaders** to lead teams; meet with them once a week to focus on grade-level and subject-area instruction. Principal meets with team leaders once a quarter to check on work and address concerns.

Team leaders meet with **teachers** once a week to discuss learning objectives and student achievement data and to determine next steps.

team leaders whether they wanted me to attend a PLC meeting, assuring them that it wouldn't hurt my feelings if they would rather proceed without me. In most cases, they were just fine without me. When they did need my help—for example, in reexamining grouping for a particular math rotation without compromising the school's mission—I was there.

Action Items

All the theory and research in the world mean nothing if they are not applied successfully. By setting up the structures, expectations, and climate for authentic instructional leadership, the educational leader can maximize the work of the professional learning community. It is the leader who ultimately clarifies the vision, facilitates joint ownership of goals, decides how time and resources are allocated, and determines the purpose, direction, and leadership of meetings.

Build a Collaborative Schedule

By building a schedule that incorporates blocks of time for collaboration, the leader can foster valuable dialogue that focuses on learning targets, student achievement, and next steps. Each school tackles schedule building differently, but the following steps will promote fairness, discussion, and reflection:

1. **Empower teachers to build the schedule.** As an elementary school principal, I assembled a scheduling committee led by a lead arts teacher and made up of several other teachers and specialists to ensure ownership and multiple perspectives, and I arranged for a full-day planning period for the committee to focus on the schedule.

2. **Articulate priorities.** I laid out a few specific parameters by articulating to the committee our shared priorities—for example, 20-minute common blocks for the morning meeting, 30-minute extended-learning blocks for 4th grade, no more morning arts for 1st grade, and so on.

3. **Emphasize equity.** Teachers and leaders can quickly size up inequity—"He has more planning time!" or "Our grade always gets stuck with language arts at the end of the day!"—so this should be closely monitored by the principal and the scheduling committee to maintain appropriate balance from year to year.

4. **Emphasize common planning time.** Ensuring that all classes in a particular grade level are attending music, art, or P.E. at the same time provides the grade-level or department teachers with shared planning time. Building in this planning time at least once a week is not only feasible but should also be a priority of the schedule committee.

5. **Conduct a final review.** Even after the committee's careful work, I would sometimes find a glitch or catch something that required follow-up. I would simply send my feedback to the committee (or lead teacher) to review and address the problem.

6. **Share the process and the product.** Each year, I shared the completed schedule with all staff members at the same time, highlighting our articulated priorities and describing the schedule-building process. I also invited any interested teachers to let me know if they wanted to help in future years' schedule committee sessions. Being open about the process and the product helps ensure staff respect and buy-in.

Share a Common Format for Minutes

Using a shared format for taking the minutes of team meetings (see Figure 2.2 for an example) allows for clarity and consistency in use of time. All teams use the same structure and submit reports weekly to the department head

Figure 2.2 | **Sample PLC Minutes Form**

PLC Minutes	
Subject/grade level: **Members present:**	**Date of meeting:** **Minutes submitted by:**
Content-area strand discussed	
Data indicators	(attach roster and indicators)
Next steps for students who are succeeding	
Next steps for students who are struggling	
Questions/issues needing further clarity	
Plan for next meeting (next strands to be covered)	

(or, in a smaller school, the relevant administrator). Team members should take turns taking the minutes. The principal should review the minutes and, when possible, provide feedback to the teams. The team member taking the minutes might even request that the principal or a division subject-area coordinator attend a PLC meeting with a particular relevant focus.

Involve Staff in Schoolwide Progress Reviews

Every school should hold midyear reviews during which the professional learning communities come together to look at and reflect on the school's current state—including areas where progress has been made and areas where there is need for growth. Although some districts mandate and even supervise these reviews, they should be school-directed, staff-owned initiatives that address the four essential PLC questions. The progress review itself is not to be evaluative but informative. It should provide an understanding of current achievement data, allow for sharing among PLCs, and highlight successes. Affirmation provides an important boost, particularly at the midpoint of the year, and it should be continually emphasized in an age of accountability that is often perceived as all doom and gloom.

Conduct Peer Observations for Leaders and Teachers

While the educational leader works to foster a positive learning climate in his or her building or division, he or she must also continue to grow and develop as an instructional leader. It has often been said—including in this book!—that leadership is carried out in solitude. However, it does not have to be that way. As an elementary school principal, I partnered with a high school principal to share strategies and solve problems (Sterrett & Haas, 2009). We collaborated in a way that was relevant and immediate. We brought each other coffee, and we walked through our schools and classrooms together. It was valuable learning, rooted in instructional leadership.

We instituted this practice at our schools as well, building in structures to allow teachers to systematically visit other classrooms to observe a specific "menu item" (such as a word wall, an effective math transition, or an art

Figure 2.3 | **Peer Observation Collaborative Slip**

Date of visit: Classroom visited: Name:	Notes and Thoughts
What I had hoped to see	
What I liked	
Further questions and ideas to think about	

Source: From "Using Technology and Teamwork to Enhance Peer Observations," by W. Sterrett, B. Williams, and J. Catlett, 2010, *Virginia Educational Leadership, 7*(1), pp. 65–71. © 2010 by Virginia ASCD. Adapted with permission.

lesson) that they could reflect on and discuss (Sterrett, Williams, & Catlett, 2010). Through the vein of trust, we asked that they share their feedback with one another, not with us as administrators (see Figure 2.3 for a sample peer observation form). Teachers had nothing but good things to say about these peer observations.

Success for All

As I discuss in the next chapter, although we often discuss education in terms of groups, we work in the business of individuals. By modeling professional learning community work in all aspects of their leadership, today's educational leaders can learn and lead in a way that bolsters the work of the school community while keeping each student in mind.

In-the-Field Activities

1. Attend a grade-level PLC (or equivalent) meeting. Pay attention to how the participants discuss

   a. The content being learned.
   b. Student achievement data.
   c. Next steps.

   Highlight which of the above items are discussed and how. Make a list of recommendations for the next meeting.

2. Reflect on your current position and your own professional growth goals. If you could spend one hour each month with a professional learning partner, who would it be? Consider a partner who is in a slightly different position than your current one (for instance, as a middle school assistant principal you might choose an elementary school principal or a high school assistant principal). Reach out to the person and see if he or she is interested in meeting monthly, alternating sites, to find ways to grow together as professionals. Here are some items you may want to include in your monthly meetings:

   a. Success stories.
   b. An instructional challenge.
   c. Walk-through observations.
   d. A professional article or book that has guided your reflection in the past month.
   e. Goals for the semester, the school year, and the next five years.

3. Which leadership traits should be embodied by the team leader, department head, or administrator? Are these traits present? If not, how would you recommend reaching these ideals?

4. As a leader, how do you know how other PLCs are conducting their meetings? Do you ever have a vertical or cross-discussion (e.g., department to department or one grade level to the next) to share ideas and discussion points? If not, how might you build such discussions into your meeting approach?

5. Review the Action Items from this chapter and develop a plan to implement at least one in your school setting. What steps do you need to take to build a collaborative schedule at your school? How could you incorporate or strengthen schoolwide progress reviews? How might peer observations strengthen the instructional focus of your learning community? What steps are needed, and how will you communicate them to your team? What challenges do you anticipate? How will you reflect on your work after implementation?

3

Turning Professional
Development into
Meaningful Growth

If you let it, this job will eat you alive; it is endless.
You have got to carve out time for growth.

—Alex Carter

Action Items
* Use meeting exit slips
* Get off campus
* Take a collaborative learning walk
* Present, publish, and advocate
* Protect personal time to avoid burnout

Continued Growth as a Leader, as a Learner

Alex Carter, a Milken National Educator and coauthor of *The Insider's Guide to High School*, spoke bluntly with me about the importance of growing as a leader: "The work is endless. What can happen is burnout, even for the most energetic principal with a strong sense of mission. I realized early on as a principal, you can work 80 hours a week and still have work to do. You have to carve out time to grow in order to remain an upbeat, positive, and effective leader."

Carter, who most recently served as the principal at Telluride High School in Telluride, Colorado, emphasizes the importance of learning at conferences, presenting to other educators, and writing and researching as a practitioner: "It's easy to lose the forest for the trees when you are running a school. You can lose sight of your original mission. You must keep your perspective and keep others around you focused. You're so focused on tardies, student discipline, schedules, lunch lines, and all the managerial items that you forget about teaching and learning."

Professional development is crucial for educators at all levels. As researchers (Wei, Darling-Hammond, & Adamson, 2010) observe in a recent National Staff Development Council report, "Without ratcheting up support for effective educator learning, the ability of teachers and school leaders to meet these new challenges will be diminished" (p. ii). The report also notes that "while U.S. policy initiatives increasingly reflect an understanding that effective teaching and school leadership are critical to the quality of education that students receive, there is often less recognition that teacher professional development is a key element of school reform" (p. 1). Thus, the onus will likely fall on the school leader to ensure meaningful growth.

As educational leaders, we are rarely given time to read, reflect, and mull over needed changes. If we want continual growth, we must seek it out. Schmoker (1999) observes that "schools improve when purpose and effort unite. One key is leadership that recognizes its most vital function: to keep everyone's eyes on the prize of improved student learning" (p. 111). Yet unless school leaders are deliberate about continuing their own learning as well as that of their staffs, they and the organizations they lead will stagnate. Principal

Carter relentlessly pursues continual professional growth. Although his priority is to help his school meet its goals, he has also set personal goals to grow as a principal.

Refresh and Retool with Staff

Even with an experienced staff, leaders must find time to cycle in "refreshers" to help staff grow. Cotton (2003) notes that principals who are successful instructional leaders offer "not only more activities [to staff] but also a wider range of them, both in terms of structure and content," and that the activities' content ranges "from general to subject-specific pedagogical skills, subject-area content, and process skills such as decision making and problem solving" (p. 36). In my own experience, I have seen schools and divisions realize continued success by emphasizing the following activities for teachers:

Content-area development. Focusing on specific strategies and approaches in a content area will always be timely and relevant. Schedule an expert in the field (ideally, a practitioner) to visit the school and address issues like these:

- **How to manage a specific teaching strategy.** A refresher on word study could benefit even the most adept veteran teachers and foster stimulating and collaborative conversation.
- **How to find updated materials and resources.** Middle school science teachers might discuss new lab materials for teaching Newton's laws, for example, or an updated WebQuest engine on the solar system.

Classroom community building. As I discuss in Chapter 5, addressing ways to build classroom community, deal with problem scenarios, and affirm students is an opportunity to arm teachers with practical, student-centered tools that will ultimately maximize instructional time.

Technology integration. It is difficult to keep up with technology without seeing real-time, relevant applications. A lead teacher or division coordinator should take time to highlight time-saving tips, practical strategies, and updated student-centered modules for teachers. Unlike many professional development sessions, such activities provide teachers with real takeaways that they appreciate.

Overcoming Challenges

"I was spending 80, 85 hours a week working at school or at school functions and I still never felt that I was getting it done," says Carter. "Even if you have a strong engine, a clear vision, the burnout factor is there. You need separation from the 'brass tacks' [so you can] actually remember what your mission is. I need perspective for me and to help others stay focused on this work." Here's how leaders can surmount several key barriers to make the important work of teaching and learning happen.

Establish Meeting Norms

Meeting norms might seem basic, but they are glaringly absent in many schools. Quite simply, meetings should begin and end on time—period. Establish and stick to a consistent time, and folks will honor these parameters. Other norms to consider include banning the use of computers or phones during meetings, setting guidelines on how to insert a question or comment into the discussion, and showing respect for others' thoughts. Post the agreed-upon norms in a prominent place and refer to them at the beginning of meetings to make sure everyone is on the same page.

Overcome the Five-Year Freeze

Carter has observed some teachers "locking in" after five years and reaching a plateau in terms of professional growth. "You have to work hard to engage and overcome resistance," he advises. Knowing where your teachers are in terms of their own development and goals is crucial in designing appropriate, targeted professional development.

State a Clear Agenda

Setting up time for professional growth in your school community is an opportunity to grow the vision into something palpable and meaningful. By stating a clear, attainable agenda for professional development time, true school improvement—not mere minutiae—becomes the focus. Carter notes, "I've never met an educator who didn't resent professional development; while the teachers want it, they are limited for time. Teachers have hard-and-fast deadlines every day. If you are going to take from their planning time, they will resent it." Carter clearly defines (1) when the professional development will happen and (2) what it will look like. There should be no substantive surprises when educators are giving up their most treasured resource—time—for professional development. As an educator, I often knew a lesson had been successful when a student could tell me the importance of the learning objective in his or her own words. Similarly, when asked, a teacher should be able to state what he or she is learning about in a given meeting.

Action Items

In their book *Techniques in the Clinical Supervision of Teachers,* Acheson and Gall (1992) note that today's leader "has to deal with the full range of personality types. These range from aggressive to passive, from authoritarian to laissez-faire, from any extreme to its opposite" (p. 214). And principals face challenges that go beyond personalities. They may feel as though they are herding cats, given the range of emotions, stages in professional growth, and current challenges that staff members bring to faculty meetings. The leader must keep colleagues' full range of needs in mind as he or she strives to maximize professional development throughout the year and remember that even the most loyal and motivated teachers have days filled with frustration, failure, or fatigue that are likely to cloud their outlook and affect their participation in a professional development session. Fortunately, several practices can help.

Use Meeting Exit Slips

Several veteran teachers told me they appreciated the opportunity, after a faculty meeting, to complete an exit slip. One even quipped that exit slips would reduce "teacher lounge grumbling" because they eliminate participants' need to rehash their thoughts later. Figure 3.1 depicts an exit slip that I found helpful for faculty meetings.

Figure 3.1 | **Faculty Meeting Exit Slip**

1. What did you find helpful about today's meeting?

2. What did you not find helpful?

3. What else would you like to learn about this topic?

4. What other questions or comments do you have?

Get Off Campus

It is difficult for educators to resist attending to e-mails that need to be answered, bulletin boards that need to be designed, and papers that need to be graded. Carter advocates setting up an off-campus retreat: "Find a meeting place where everyone can focus. This could even be a neighboring school building: principals can swap buildings and focus on the work. There is a 500-yard rule—if teachers are within 500 yards of their classrooms, they simply cannot stop thinking about what they need to do in their classrooms and what they are going to do tomorrow. This physical separation is a must as our teachers are thinking of the various deadlines that they need to accomplish."

Take a Collaborative Learning Walk

"The sit-and-get approach does not work," Carter observes. Teachers do not want another college lecture; they want something useful and memorable that helps them move toward goals that are relevant and timely. The district should promote a sense of shared ownership and accountability with its teachers and principals. As a principal, I cringed when I read of schools that didn't make adequate yearly progress having their principals reassigned, or worse. Some may ask, "Where are the division 'cubicle coordinators' and other leaders when schools do not meet the mark? Are they safe simply because they don't work with kids?" Although these questions may sound cynical, they are on many teachers' and principals' minds.

This largely inaccurate perception can be eliminated by having school and division leaders work alongside teachers in initiatives that help the school meet its accountability goals. Carter and his teacher colleagues take frequent collaborative learning walks, visiting classrooms to watch learning unfold, to ask questions, and to offer affirmation and feedback. Like the peer observation approach I discuss in Chapter 2, this practice provides the greater school community with a valuable look at learning in the school. Reeves (2008) notes that "the direct observation of the professional practices of teachers by teachers must become the new foundation of professional development" (p. 3). Figure 3.2 shows a sample learning walk observation and feedback sheet.

Present, Publish, and Advocate

Today's teacher leaders and principals have much to contribute as voices in the field. Carter notes that "sharing with others in the field 'fills up my cup,' as I receive valuable feedback" in return. Most states and all regional areas have professional organizations that rely on current practitioners to speak at their annual conferences and write for their publications. By merging theory and practice in a reflective and engaging manner (as I did in articles for such magazines as *Educational Leadership* and *Principal*), you will realize that you have a lot to share with and learn from colleagues across the nation. Writing takes time, but it is well worth the effort to see your work in print. More important, it opens up doors for meaningful dialogue. School leaders must understand the big-picture forces that shape our world: federal and state law (including court decisions), local finance and budget implications, and testing and accountability mandates that influence the work in our schools. By staying involved in organizations with a policy emphasis, such as ASCD and Kappa Delta Pi, educators can help shape these vital conversations.

Protect Personal Time to Avoid Burnout

In an age of increasing accountability and workload, today's leaders must protect their own personal time. As Carter insists, "You've got to stay sane." Set a goal to leave by a certain time each day. As an elementary school teacher with an arrival time of 7 a.m., my departure time was 4:45 p.m. Of course,

---

Figure 3.2 | **Collaborative Learning Walk Notes**

Today the learning walk team did a short, "down-and-dirty" visit of five classrooms. Once again the team enjoyed the classroom visits and felt that the overall climate of the building was positive and moving in the right direction. As always, good relationships between students and teachers were in evidence. We all felt that there was plenty to celebrate on this walk. Today I will highlight three "glows" and two "grows."

Glows

1. We loved the way Jane Jones used self-progress monitoring in her classroom. As she begins every period for her writing class, students do a timed typing exercise. At the end of the exercise, students self-report their results in a group format on the whiteboard. Students then enter all the data into an Excel spreadsheet. Then they look at their own personal progress and the progress of the class as a whole by averaging the scores and comparing them with the previous day's scores. We like this because it hit on so many different best practices. Student self-progress monitoring is a research-based strategy to motivate students to work harder. This exercise multiplied the strategy's impact by reinforcing the students' Excel spreadsheet skills and their basic math skills and competencies. Well done, Jane!

2. We loved the way Sam Smith and John Doe have made classroom procedures such a seamless and integral part of their classroom culture, allowing students to engage in experiential learning while never seeming to be in chaos. We remarked that it was neat to see 20 different students working on 20 different projects in Emily Jones's class, and all feeling supported. Very nice!

3. We saw lots of smooth transitions in evidence in nearly every classroom we visited. Not once did we hear a student say, "What are we doing again?" or see students looking around in confusion. This shows that students are comfortable and keenly aware of what they are doing. This is a hallmark of competent instruction and class management.

Grows

1. Although the students clearly know what they are expected to be doing, there still is little evidence that they have an absolutely concrete and clear

---

Figure 3.2 (continued) | **Collaborative Learning Walk Notes**

vision of *what* they are supposed to be learning, *why* the learning is important and how it fits into the overall schema for the class, and *how* they will
be assessed for mastery. Certainly there was no visual evidence of a clear
learning objective in each of the rooms we visited. I encourage you to read
the great synopsis from the Marshall Memo I sent yesterday that addressed
the importance of developing and communicating a clear purpose for every
lesson.

2. We saw evidence of several great product/project/performance assessments as we walked around the building. In all cases, the students were
   aware of the elements that they would be expected to demonstrate in order
   to submit a complete work. What we didn't see, however, were clear and
   articulated rubrics of how each element would be scored. When we asked
   the students if they thought they were doing *A*-quality work, they usually
   replied, "I hope so." Well-developed rubrics are a standards-based and
   research-supported practice. Please use them.

Once again, thank you for allowing us into your classrooms for our learning
walk. If you haven't yet participated in a learning walk this semester, there are
three more chances:

- November 11—5th period
- November 17—6th period
- December 2—7th period

Please sign up on the Doodle for your spot on the team!

Best regards,

Alex Carter, Principal

you will often have evening events, school board meetings, PTO meetings, community college class presentations, and other events that pepper your calendar. I also advise turning off your handheld phone each evening and waiting until the next day to respond to calls and e-mails. Admittedly, this is difficult advice to follow. But I realized that once I started checking and answering work-related e-mails from my living room, I was suddenly back at school—and it affected my perspective and mood. In his early years as a principal, Carter learned this lesson from a colleague who advised him to "always take a vacation, and leave the electronics off."

A Catalyst for Engagement and Success

Professional development is necessary and, if used in an authentic and engaging manner, can serve as a catalyst in helping collaborative teams realize their goals. Doug Reeves (2009) notes that "leaders set the direction of the professional development agenda. Unfortunately, some schools are still influenced by vendors who cram every available second of professional development time with mind-numbing workshops" (p. 63). School leaders should seek to engage and challenge the minds of educators. By ensuring that this work is targeted, clear, and collaborative, leaders will provide an experience that refreshes the faculty in much-needed areas and enables them to conquer challenges together in a meaningful, lasting way. Find a time and a place to remove yourself from the phone calls, e-mails, and papers that need grading. Focus on your work . . . *together*. Reflect and share feedback. Those buses will be back, and your work will be waiting for you.

In-the-Field Activities

1. Revisit your meeting norms. Which norms ensure consistency, fairness, and adherence to the agenda items? Discuss and develop a list of norms as a staff and post them in a prominent location. At the beginning of each meeting, be sure to refer to them.

2. Consider an innovative initiative that you have helped lead for your team, school, or division. How might you share this work in a state, regional, or national presentation or publication? Pick three possible forums (start with www.ascd.org as a resource and research your state chapter) in which you might share ideas that are relevant for today's educators.

3. Consider a "500-yard" location that is at least a short walk away from your usual meeting designation at school. How can you arrange an off-campus meeting? How might you structure this meeting to engage participants in significant, meaningful work?

4. Review the Action Items from this chapter and develop a plan to implement at least one in your school setting. At the end of your next meeting, allow five minutes for participants to fill out an exit slip. What feedback did you get? What changes will you make in the future? How might exit slips enhance your meetings? Take several teacher leaders on a learning walk through the school building. Think of other ways to "share out from within" the learning strategies you observe.

Section 2

Strengthening
the Learning Community

4

Turning Differentiated
Learning and Leading into
Success for All

Let's look at who people are and what they can do instead
of focusing so much on what they can't do.

—*Carol Ann Tomlinson*

Action Items
* Listen to different voices in staff
  meetings
* Hire as a team
* Provide relevant professional
  development
* Rethink discipline
* Recognize staff success
* Recognize student success

A Teacher in Touch

Dr. Carol Ann Tomlinson, a renowned educator and best-selling author of *The Differentiated Classroom,* advocates an approach in which "teachers are more in touch with their students and approach teaching more as an art than as a mechanical exercise" (1999, p. 8). I spoke with Tomlinson about her insights; rather than proposing any specific formula, Tomlinson advises educators to look for "where folks need to end up, understand where they are now, and find ways to help students get there." She believes that differentiated instruction is a "natural outgrowth of burgeoning understanding of the ways children learn" (1999, p. 17).

"Temple Grandin is Exhibit A in differentiated learning," Tomlinson explains, "because she has profoundly different ways of learning, yet she has tremendous capacity to learn. She really needed someone to ask, 'How can we unleash the potential that is there and help her show us what can work for her, and how do we develop ways to get her where she needs to go?'"

Currently a professor in the Animal Sciences Department at Colorado State University, Temple Grandin is well known for being a prominent voice for people with autism, and she was the subject of the award-winning biographical movie that bears her name. In her book *Thinking in Pictures* (1995), Temple Grandin explains, "I think in pictures. Words are like a second language to me. I translate both spoken and written words into full-color movies, complete with sound, which run like a VCR tape in my head" (p. 19).

I interviewed Temple Grandin because she is unique and because she benefited from a teacher who saw that uniqueness as a gift. Grandin credits her teachers for seeing her as an individual learner and reaching her in unique ways: "I had very good elementary school teachers and a science teacher in high school, Mr. Carlock, who was a very creative guy" (personal communication, 2010). Effective teachers were able to reach Grandin "because they showed me that if I wanted to learn about something like the squeeze machine, then I had to learn the science around it." When she became a teacher herself, Grandin realized that her students relied on different types of thinking and that she, too, needed to learn to meet the individual needs of learners rather than using a one-size-fits-all approach.

The Right Fit for Students

To succeed, students need to be seen as individuals. This may seem like a tall order for a teacher guiding a classroom of 29 learners. Nevertheless, the only way for teachers to meet all their students' needs is to continually take the pulse of each learner and understand that each one is unique. Despite their differences, with the right guidance, students will find the "right fit" within the classroom environment as they meet new and exciting challenges. Similarly, teachers can find their own right fit as essential members of their PLCs and the greater school community.

Keeping a Finger on the Pulse

Effective teachers continually have their finger on the pulse of the students in their classrooms. As school leaders, we should emphasize regular diagnostic assessments conducted in a way that informs instruction. In Chapter 8, I discuss the importance of assessment in more detail, but taking an initial inventory of your school's current state will inform you where students are and help you ensure a clear, deliberate, and balanced approach to grouping, instruction, and assessment of students.

Clarity and Persistence

Clarity and persistence are always evident in a successful school, says Tomlinson. She has seen effective school leaders who "were not going to let the initiative go away. They did not see a spurt and then a level, but continued growth. They were there day after day, week after week, year after year," ensuring that the work continued. The teacher must be clear about what is to be taught and when it is to be taught, and the administrator should consistently ensure that the "what" and the "when" are not compromised. This is not to say that all teachers must be on the same page of a basal reader on a specific day, but teachers should follow a quarterly pacing guide that ensures that material is being covered. Still, it is important that the school leader respect teacher autonomy and be flexible on the "how" of the teaching.

Understanding That Students Are Different

Temple Grandin's teachers took stock of her interests and engaged her in creative ways. Similarly, today's educators need to be aware of each of the 20-plus students in their classrooms and keep in mind that each student is different. While holding firm on classroom expectations and learning objectives, teachers need to find different ways to engage different students, and school leaders should work to facilitate growth in this important area. "Teachers must come to believe that all students can grow," says Tomlinson. Students need to understand, she emphasizes, that "it's not that some students in the class are smart and some aren't or that some are going to succeed and some aren't but that everyone is going to be successful and we are going to find out how to make that happen."

Becoming a school that truly values different learning styles and strives to meet the needs of all students is no easy task. However, with clarity and perseverance, educational leaders in the field have embraced diverse student populations and witnessed great success. A differentiated classroom will engage students, regardless of their current achievement level, in an appropriate learning activity that challenges them to grow and respond to and interact with the learning environment. The students in such a classroom will understand the objective and what the outcomes should be; they will be given the opportunity to have a voice in what is learned and, most important, how they will learn it.

The Right Fit in Leadership

Differentiation is also essential in leadership. In her work, Tomlinson has found that successful principals lead with a differentiated approach specific to their schools' needs. What they all have in common is a "real sense of vision and mission" that they keep "in front of people consistently. They play a large role in the ongoing growth of teachers, constantly in the classroom, listening and questioning, and are extremely involved in the process."

Unique People, Unique Needs

As educational leaders, we must be willing to see staff members, situations, and contexts as unique. A one-size-fits-all approach simply does not work in most leadership situations. As Duke (2010) notes, "Schools function in different contexts and face different challenges. These differences call for school leaders to differentiate their priorities, theories of action, and ways of leading" (p. 2). Organizational theory bears out this assertion. De Greene (1982) notes that contingency theory is essential to understanding how organizations run because they involve "complex interrelationships among environmental certainty and diversity, internal differentiation and integration, and conflict resolution" (p. 25). In their book *Differentiated Leadership,* Kise and Russell (2008) advise leaders to understand their own personality types and encourage staff to do the same to foster a multifaceted approach to working together in an organization.

As Jim Collins (2001) famously noted in *Good to Great,* the right fit also requires having "the right people on the bus" (p. 13). Assembling the right team requires vision and purposeful planning. It is important to recruit and retain people who will help the organization realize its vision in a productive and professional manner. Duke (2010) notes that a "key element in developing a capable staff is recruitment. School leaders must be clear about the kinds of expertise needed to serve their students and then identify the places where they are most likely to find it" (p. 96).

The Relational Component

Successful leaders understand that relationships are key in leading, learning, and living as an educator. As Michael Fullan (2001) notes, "You can't get anywhere without them. . . . It's the *relationships* that make the difference" (p. 51). Fullan asserts that a relational understanding of people is essential to an organization's success, noting that although the "knowledge, skills, and dispositions of teachers as *individuals* is obviously important and can make a difference in individual classrooms, schools must also focus on creating schoolwide *professional learning communities*" (p. 64). Authentic relationships enable professional learning communities to thrive in an environment of collaboration and trust, they help teachers to build community within their classrooms and focus on learning rather than discipline, and they allow colleagues to grow professionally and become stronger educators.

Relationships are vitally important in the business of education because it takes a team to do this work. No division leader, principal, or teacher can bear the full responsibility. As Doug Reeves (2009) notes, "Of all the variables that influence student achievement, the two that have the most profound influence are teacher quality and leadership quality" (p. 67). Quality teaching and quality leadership go hand in hand in meeting the needs of a diverse learning organization and are both essential for the lasting success of both students and staff members. Having the right people on the bus and ensuring that they are working together in a healthy manner will enable the organization to meet and conquer challenges that arise.

Overcoming Challenges

Fostering a culture of differentiation and fairness is a worthy ideal, but not one that's necessarily easy to translate into action. We must emphasize and model leadership that ensures that each student—from the disengaged, struggling student to the motivated prodigy—is being challenged to reach new heights. Similarly, we must encourage our staff members to contribute to and lead in an environment that values quality instruction and shared ownership.

Require Clarity and Persistence

As discussed previously in this chapter, clarity and persistence are key to success. Tomlinson notes that the successful leaders she has worked with "really didn't do much different from what books on leadership tell you to do. They just did it. . . . Successful change often takes a number of years. A leader needs to know what they want to do, why they want to do it, and be willing to go the journey."

Persistence, regardless of a particular school's makeup, is essential to ensuring that differentiation indeed occurs. According to Tomlinson and her coauthor Jay McTighe (2006), answering "yes" to the following three questions will promote successful differentiation:

1. Do we have the will and skill to accept responsibility for the diverse individuals we teach?

2. Do we have a vision of the power of high-quality learning to help young people build lives?

3. Are we willing to do the work of building bridges of possibility between what we teach and the diverse learners we teach? (pp. 56–57)

Form Fair Judgments . . . *On Your Own*

We should hold our staffs to a high standard. Yet we should also realize that staff members are often grappling with unhealthy stress levels, varied professional goals, and difficult situations within the workplace. When we assume a position of leadership, we will undoubtedly hear the scoop of which staff members are effective, which are "dead weight," which are "drama-prone," and so on. Rather than take these estimations at face value, we should reach our own conclusions through observation and time. Being new provides a wonderful opportunity to conduct formal and informal observations and gather actual data rather than rely on hearsay. When a difficult personnel situation does arise, we must not jump to conclusions but instead seek to understand the circumstance, hear from all parties involved, weigh the facts, and reflect carefully before acting. This is true for our work with both students and staff. Perceptions are not always accurate, and we must remain mindful that the people we work with, as well as the situations that crop up, are all unique and require professional judgment and carefully thought-out responses.

Action Items

School leaders, juggling as we do improvement goals, organizational demands, and a variety of situational contexts while working with multiple stakeholders, are certainly familiar with complex interrelationships. In the complicated enterprise of schooling, a proactive approach is a must. Tomlinson notes that "the whole point of differentiation is to look at who people are and what they can do instead of focusing on what they can't do and to find the strengths and avenues that do work for people." A leader may need to vary his or her approach to recognize and capitalize on the diverse strengths of the organization while also working to optimize consistency and coherence. Luckily, flexibility and consistency are not mutually exclusive; here are some examples of how a leader can incorporate both.

Listen to Different Voices in Staff Meetings

Students learn and communicate in different ways, and adults are no different. Structuring a faculty meeting to include a handful of 45-second "teaching snapshots" of engaged learning throughout the building affirms faculty members and shows them a diverse array of instructional strategies that they may miss in isolation. By incorporating games and interactive sharing in our meetings, we give all staff an opportunity to be heard.

Hire as a Team

Hiring should be a team decision. By forming representative teams, the educational leader can prioritize essential "look-fors" during the hiring process while also allowing the applicant to learn about the diverse perspectives of the staff. Rather than hiring ideologically similar, cookie-cutter candidates, the leader should emphasize various learning and leading styles while not compromising on essentials, such as putting students first, following through on objectives, and working well with others. This approach will also foster buy-in from existing staff members, who have a stake in seeing that the newly hired team member succeeds.

Provide Relevant Professional Development

Tomlinson believes that school leaders should model differentiated learning through professional development: "Anything we want the teachers to do in the classroom, we should do with them as well." Tomlinson notes that teachers will be sold on differentiated instruction when they themselves are taught in an individualized way that emphasizes the following key points:

- **Clarify desired outcomes.** Just as teachers do for students, leaders should ascertain which knowledge and skills are most important for their learning populations (i.e., staffs) to obtain and then clearly lay out their expectations.

- **Assess and approach.** Pre-assess to see where teachers are and then set out to support them in a systematic way, continually keeping an eye out for strengths and gaps.
- **Foster collaboration.** Working together is essential. According to Tomlinson, leaders must believe and maintain the assumption that "we are all going to get there" as an organization, but the school needs to make collaboration a way of life to reach its goals.

Rethink Discipline

Certain disciplinary practices such as zero-tolerance policies should be reexamined. During my first week as an administrator, I heard a kindergarten student unleash a string of expletives as he stepped off the bus. While some might argue for school handbook–sanctioned consequences such as suspension, it was essential that I first considered the context. "Where did he learn those words? Why was he using them? What did he mean?" Suspending a kindergarten student during his first week of school for saying something he had likely not learned at school would serve no gain. But explaining to him that those were not words we used at school and asking his teacher to reinforce appropriate expressions would help him learn how to be a part of our school community. Often, our most vulnerable or at-risk students suffer the most severe consequences, which just thrusts them back into an unsafe environment.

Recognize Staff Success

Duke (2010) believes that principals must notch some "quick wins" to bolster the confidence of the staff, observing that "every school, no matter how low-performing, has some positive aspects" and that it is "important for school leaders to understand why certain aspects of the school are working reasonably well" (p. 64).

Consider making substantial, clearly noticed improvements in a few key areas, including meeting with faculty to gain their input and build trust, providing instructional materials in an efficient and effective way, and making schedule tweaks that benefit students and staff alike. Leaders should also honor staff success. By recognizing the diversity of the team while affirming its shared successes, a supportive leader can use celebrations to lighten the work environment in a positive way.

Recognize Student Success

A principal should also carve out time to recognize student achievements. Here are a couple of ideas:

- **Bulletin Board Wall of Fame.** Capture work in the classroom or school and personalize the achievement with a notation. For instance, displaying students' written accounts of their field trip to a local cavern with a small note written by the teacher that explains the trip and corresponding assignment can brighten up the hallway and provide an example of a learning experience that occurs outside the walls of the school.
- **Student of the Week.** By celebrating students who show improvement, marked academic success, or good citizenship, the principal can electrify Friday morning announcements by announcing the students' accomplishments and handing each an individualized certificate. When I was a principal, after I had read students' names over the PA system, they would usually show up in the office within minutes to pick up their awards, beaming with pride.

Staying in Balance

As leaders, we must ensure that we maintain balance in our own lives. Being the first one to arrive and the last one to leave rarely impresses anyone; it instead signals that the leader is either too harried to get it together or simply a workaholic who may have unreasonable expectations of his or her colleagues. Leaders should work as hard as anyone, but we should also model and reflect balance, moderation, and a healthy perspective for the entire organization. As Kise and Russell (2008) point out in *Differentiated Leadership*, we should all take stock of our own personality types as well as those in our organization and occasionally check ourselves to ensure that we are not falling out of balance and causing undue stress to others.

In-the-Field Activities

1. Find out, through a division instructional leader, the names of two teachers (preferably at two different levels—for example, elementary school and high school) who are effective at differentiating in their classrooms. Schedule an observation with them and describe what you see.

2. Summarize the steps required to plan an effective differentiated lesson. How does the teacher introduce the topic? How does he or she facilitate movement and engagement and keep a finger on the pulse of the learning in the classroom? How does he or she bring it all together at the end of the class?

3. What are some quick wins that you could make in your school or department to "secure support of teachers and community members" (Duke, 2010, p. 62) and show that progress can and will be made? Duke offers the following quick wins (pp. 62–66) as targets:

   a. Student behavior: What expectations and procedures can your school adopt and consistently apply to help improve student behavior?

   b. Student attendance: What steps can your school take to bolster student attendance?

   c. Faculty commitment: How might you solicit authentic, relevant input from colleagues that enhances your perspective and builds trust?

   d. Environmental improvements: What unsightly areas around the building and grounds could be targeted for quick, low-cost, but noticeable improvements?

   e. Instructional materials: How can you cut through the red tape and get some sorely needed materials for your students and staff?

   f. Schedule adjustments: Are there any adjustments you could make to the master schedule that would bolster instructional time and improve climate?

4. Review the Action Items from this chapter and develop a plan to implement at least one in your school setting. How can you incorporate different voices into your faculty meetings in a meaningful way? How can you be mindful of the need for different perspectives in hiring new staff members? What are some ways you can ensure that professional development is meaningful to the different members of your staff? What are some different ways of recognizing success from within your learning community? What challenges do you anticipate? How will you reflect on your work after implementation?

5

From Discipline
to Relationships

Building relationships is key to building a positive learning
community. Spending time on social and emotional
learning enables academic gains to happen.

—Roxann Kriete

Action Items
* Communicate a common vision with
  clear goals
* Equip your toolbox
* Hold a Morning Meeting
* Add a safety layer of support
* Form preemptive relationships

The Silent Bulldozer of School Reform

Author and former high school teacher Roxann Kriete is known for her book *The Morning Meeting Book,* in which she articulates the power of starting the day with a Morning Meeting. This "silent bulldozer of school reform" (2002, p. 135) enables teachers and students to work together to build social and emotional foundations that maximize teaching and learning for all. As a practitioner, Kriete is a realist, acknowledging the roles and responsibilities that teachers have to juggle to do their jobs. She is also a fierce advocate for children. She recalls how a former student contacted her to note the profound impact Kriete had made on her simply by saying hello to her each day: "It made me feel like it really mattered that I came" (p. 1). The Morning Meeting strategy, developed at the Northeast Foundation for Children, involves a 30-minute meeting each morning during which students greet one another, share news of interest, engage in a group activity, and listen to news and announcements. This particular approach has had a positive influence on many schools by making students realize that they do, in fact, matter very much.

From early childhood through the rambunctious teen years, each classroom must make students feel connected to the learning community and believe that their thoughts and contributions are important. As Christenbury (2010) writes, "Good teaching comes not from following a recipe, but from consistently putting student needs first" (p. 47). Likewise, Chenoweth (2010) urges today's educators to "be relentlessly respectful—and respectfully relentless" as they model "the way free citizens should treat one another in a democracy—with tolerance, respect, and high expectations" (p. 20). Building this community takes time and trust, but it should be the utmost priority for today's educational leader.

Students Learn from *and* for Teachers

As an administrator, I interviewed countless candidates for teaching and leadership positions in our schools. I generally was not interested in alma maters or GPAs. What mattered most was how the applicants could relate to students and engage them as learners. I wanted to hire teachers who saw students as opportunities, not discipline problems. Nothing made me cringe more than seeing a teacher reflexively send a student to the office for rolling his or her eyes, refusing to work, or committing some other classroom infraction. As I would watch the 8-year-old trudge into the office with nothing in hand but a referral, I knew that the teacher was endangering his or her own ability to connect with that student as a learner. Little, if any, learning occurs in the office or during suspension. Students need relationships built on trust and high expectations, and the best learning happens when students are engaged in the learning environment, not sent out because they do not fit in.

In *The Art and Science of Teaching,* Robert Marzano (2007) writes, "Arguably the quality of the relationships teachers have with students is the keystone of effective management and *perhaps even the entirety of teaching*" (p. 149, emphasis added). For some students, particularly those who are deemed at risk, this relational aspect is especially important. Students can be considered at risk for a variety of reasons. Current federal law defines student *subgroups* as "students with disabilities," "students with limited English proficiency," "African American students," "Hispanic students," "Native American students," and others (U.S. Department of Education, 2007, p. xxiii). Researcher Lisa Delpit (2006) makes an interesting observation: "I have discovered that children of color, particularly African American, seem especially sensitive to their relationship between themselves and their teacher. I have concluded that it appears that they learn not only from a teacher but also for a teacher. If they do not feel connected to a teacher on an emotional level, then they will not learn, they will not put out the effort" (p. 227).

This can be said for many students: the teacher must connect with them in a relational way. By forming individual relationships with students and building an interconnected classroom community, teachers can maximize instruction and student learning.

A growing body of research bears out this finding: students whose schools focus on social and emotional learning achieve at higher levels. A meta-analysis conducted by the Collaborative for Academic, Social, and Emotional

Learning of more than 300 studies involving more than 300,000 students found that when schools focused on students' social and emotional needs in a programmatic way, they saw improvements in "children's behavior, attitudes toward school, and academic achievement gains" (Payton et al., 2008, p. 8). Those of us who serve as teachers and leaders know that we teach *children,* not just subjects or grades.

"They Need to Be in School"

At the end of my first year as principal, I stood in front of the faculty and wrote a number—a large number—on the easel that is a staple in any faculty meeting. It was the number of discipline referrals we had processed throughout the year. I then wrote another large number; that was the number of out-of-school suspensions. Then I wrote down a final number: the percentage of our suspended students who were eligible for free or reduced-price lunch.

The referral and suspension numbers were much too high. Our discipline data outpaced those of the other elementary schools in our division, and our students who were deemed at risk due to socioeconomic status or other indicators were being "disciplined" by staying home from school—often to "play video games by myself," as one returning student told me. We were missing the point—big-time.

As principal, I *owned* this issue. I was the one who ultimately signed the suspension letter and told the guardian that his or her child needed to go home. This was always a difficult situation—for the guardian who had to shuffle job and supervision responsibilities, for me as a new principal trying to build community, and for the teachers who often saw their students act out even more once they learned that getting into trouble would get them out of class. We had all worked diligently in that first year to reach students, clarify our expectations, and build a system of consequences. But our students needed to be in school, in class, learning. We needed positive relationships with our students, and we needed them to know that they could succeed as learners in our school.

Overcoming Challenges

Before charging full steam ahead to establish a schoolwide practice such as the Morning Meeting, a school leader should consider several key factors within his or her own school or department. Staff members will likely hold varying opinions about climate and discipline; the leader must be prepared to build—not simply mandate—consensus. Parents, too, will likely have firmly held perceptions regarding the way the school approaches climate and discipline; principals and teachers must be willing to communicate expectations in a consistent manner. And after implementing changes, there will still be incidents, and some staff and parent concerns will remain. Yet school leaders must be willing to persevere in this important work and believe that building a strong community will yield positive gains for the school.

Avoid Initiative Fatigue

Kriete explained to me, "There is a limit to what and how much a teacher can do well at once, especially when we are asking them to try something new." Leaders must be realistic when setting goals. Kriete urges them not only to limit the number of initiatives they are launching simultaneously but also to make sure that different initiatives dovetail with one another. For example, Kriete offers, "We promote giving students choices within academic curricula, and this might not work if you are implementing a lockstep instructional program at the same time."

Make Time and Protect Time

Leaders have the power to make time for important initiatives, and they should. For example, when making a master schedule, Kriete says, "The principal can prioritize and thus enable successful Morning Meetings to be built in to the schedule." Leaders should also account for potential interruptions such as public announcements, pull-out interventions, and assemblies to protect time for the initiative.

Get Buy-In from the Community

Community members may be unaware or skeptical of a school commitment to build 20–30 minutes into the master schedule for a Morning Meeting. Inviting parents and community members to Morning Meetings and involving them actively in the meetings gets the word out and builds community. I have observed teachers inviting parents in to help with a small lesson on learning another language, to speak about their professions, or to introduce students to an interesting plant or animal.

Foster Consistency and Support

Fostering a sense of stability and consistency and providing the necessary nuts and bolts are crucial to helping a new program thrive. To implement the Morning Meeting, Kriete says that leaders should ensure that teachers have materials for the key components of the meeting, including a rug for students to gather on and a chart stand with paper. Distributing these during a professional development session will indicate commitment and support and send the message that this initiative is here to stay.

Action Items

A few strategies can help teachers build community and structure their classes to focus on learning rather than discipline. To realize success, leaders will need to look at both the big picture and the details.

Communicate a Common Vision with Clear Goals

The leader must work with the school community to cultivate, communicate, and sustain a vision that serves as the compass for stakeholders. A vision might entail a broad theme such as "engaged students learning together," but it must be supported by specific goals and programs. These are some ideas I have seen work at the school level:

- Each week, we will choose a Student of the Week to recognize students who achieve in the classroom, show improvement, or set a positive example for their peers.

- Each faculty member will make five positive phone calls every week to connect and build relationships with students' guardians.
- We will implement a common framework at the beginning of each day to allow students to come together in a purposeful way (see "Hold a Morning Meeting").
- We will have an in-class support structure for students who disrupt class or who are not engaged in learning. Using this structure, we will reduce discipline referrals by 25 percent from last year.
- We will offer a safe alternative for students who are disruptive and for whom the in-class support structure is not successful. This on-campus alternative will provide a structured time for students to cool down, refocus, engage academically, and prepare to reenter the learning environment (see "Add a Safety Layer of Support").

Equip Your Toolbox

Few of the above programs will work effectively unless the staff collectively takes time to understand the program objectives and the steps necessary to meet those objectives, to set goals, and to implement the steps correctly. Input from relevant stakeholders, such as students and colleagues throughout the building, should be valued, and the new approach should be revisited throughout the year through periodic training and discussion. As Kriete explains, "We need practical ways to reach the goals of effective school community." At the school level, teachers can use the following practices to track and communicate progress in areas that still need work:

- Keep logs of positive phone calls made to students' families.
- Make "think sheets" available that allow students to articulate their feelings and reflect on their actions while cooling down.
- After exhausting other steps, follow the school discipline referral process by writing a referral that is not angry or accusatory—sometimes, educators as well as students need a cooldown period!—but notes the steps taken and requests assistance from the administrator.

- Recognize and affirm positive behavior through a Student of the Week program at the class or schoolwide level that becomes an integral part of the weekly routine.
- Review and reinforce recess expectations. Teachers should exercise proximity to students and student activity during recess more than any other time. Often, we use recess as a time to catch up with our colleagues and watch students from afar. But I have rarely seen students make poor choices when their teacher is actively present during recess. As a teacher and as a principal, playing basketball or another game with students enabled me to connect with them, set an example for fair play and being active, and greatly reduced misbehavior.

Hold a Morning Meeting

Many schools and teachers have found success in bringing students together to learn, share news, and understand one another. Kriete explains that the Morning Meeting is a gathering that "sets the tone for the day and helps teach students positive behaviors" and enables teachers and students to "build classroom community, allow children to get to know each other. Knowing each other is a fundamental building block to work and collaborate together." In *The Morning Meeting Book,* Kriete (2002) emphasizes four cornerstone components that "gradually weave a web that binds a class together" (p. 3):

1. **Greeting.** Children greet one another by name and often engage in handshaking, clapping, singing, and other activities.

2. **Sharing.** Students share some news of interest with the class and respond to one another, articulating their thoughts, feelings, and ideas in a positive manner.

3. **Group activity.** The whole class engages in a short activity together, building class cohesion through active participation.

4. **Morning message.** Students develop language skills and learn about the events of the day ahead by reading and discussing a daily message posted for them.

Add a Safety Layer of Support

We have all witnessed unacceptable behavior that just doesn't respond to everyday interventions—a continually disruptive primary student, for example, or a middle school student who provokes a fight even after being given a warning. As I started my second year as principal, I knew that my staff and I needed to go beyond devising a common vision and classroom structures. To address more serious or stubborn misbehavior, I worked with my school division to secure a learning cottage (a trailer) and hired a full-time assistant to monitor students for a limited period of time following a disruptive event. We referred to the learning cottage as the Support Center. Although each situation was unique, this is what our general approach looked like:

1. The student goes through a cooldown period lasting no longer than 10–15 minutes. Students should complete the cooldown without distractions, away from any other students.

2. The student, with help from the assistant, completes a reflection sheet that prompts him or her to take stock of what happened; suggest alternative, more constructive behaviors or reactions; and perhaps form an apology.

3. The student completes classroom work that he or she missed by being out of class. (Sometimes we provided an alternative assignment, but our goal was to maintain what was being taught in the original learning environment.)

4. The student returns—and is welcomed—to class. The assistant escorts the student back to class, with the completed work. The student is given the opportunity to apologize, if necessary, and reenters the original learning environment. (Sterrett & JohnBull, 2009)

This safety layer of support reinforced my commitment as principal to our teachers and school community and demonstrated that we would do everything we could to offer safe alternatives that would allow us to maximize instructional time—*together*.

Form Preemptive Relationships

During my third year as principal, my colleagues and I realized that although we had made great strides in collaboratively building healthy relationships, we could do even better by matching staff members with particular students and having those staff members check in with their assigned students each week (Sterrett, Murray, & Sclater, 2011). Checking in might involve eating lunch together, tutoring, playing basketball or a board game, or going on a special trip once a semester, such as to an orchard or a bowling alley.

More than 30 staff members and 40 students participated in this program. Staff members could nominate students who they felt would benefit from having a mentor. This program worked because it was initiated by the teachers and enabled us to take a deliberate approach in reaching out to students.

Relationships Are Key

At the end of the day, students may not remember their test scores, the cafeteria food, or all their teachers' curricular choices. But they *will* remember a teacher who made a lasting impact on their lives. In our quest to maximize learning, we must never forget that a key building block is fostering a climate that allows us to teach—and reach—our students.

In-the-Field Activities

1. Examine the discipline data in your school or division. Look closely at the number of discipline referrals, suspensions, and, if possible, student data (including academic achievement level, socioeconomic status, and so on). Devise strategies to address discipline issues for all students.

2. Lead a team of teachers through the Morning Meeting format during a faculty meeting or at the outset of a professional development day. Devise a 20-minute meeting opener that includes the four components of the Morning Meeting: greeting, sharing, group activity, and

morning message. Reflect on the process following the opener and discuss how it opens up learning possibilities for both faculty and students.

3. Make a list of comments or frustrations about school climate that you hear from your colleagues. Consider how you might involve stakeholders to collaboratively address the issues.

4. Review the Action Items from this chapter and develop a plan to implement at least one in your school setting. Consider setting goals as an organization. What training would be necessary? What strategies have you seen work in your school? What support layers would demonstrate to stakeholders a shared commitment to strengthening the school community? In what ways might your school initiate pre-emptive relationships with students? What steps are needed, and how will you communicate them to your team? What challenges do you anticipate? How will you reflect on your work after implementation?

From In-Class Instruction
to Out-of-School Learning

If including nature in the daily school experience enhances health, the learning environment, and test scores, then why not find ways to do it?

—Richard Louv

Action Items
* Create ownership
* Enlist volunteers
* Highlight your nature learning initiatives
* Take schoolwide field trips
* Provide team building for staff
* Provide team building for students
* Develop thematic units
* Get outdoors, anytime, for any reason

Combating Nature-Deficit Disorder

Best-selling author Richard Louv wants us all to get outside more—*much* more. Louv, the recipient of numerous recognitions and awards, including the 2008 Audubon Medal, chairs the Children & Nature Network, which has identified and supported "more than 80 city, state, provincial, and regional campaigns focused on getting children and you out into nature" (Charles, Louv, & St. Antoine, 2010, p. 8). In his book *Last Child in the Woods*, Louv (2008) discusses the phenomenon of nature-deficit disorder, which he defines as a "growing gap between human beings and nature, with implications for health and well-being" (p. 26). In today's schools, nearly all instructional time is spent indoors. Many factors are to blame, from the standards and accountability movement to inadequate planning, safety concerns, community restrictions, and lack of access for some sites. Whatever the reasons, Louv insists that the recent push for natural school reform "is long overdue" (p. 204).

Although some children are particularly drawn to the natural world as a facet of the naturalist intelligence posited by Howard Gardner (1999), research (Charles & Louv, 2009) increasingly indicates that *all* students could benefit from a greater emphasis on environment-based education. Louv explains that "researchers have demonstrated that student achievement levels rise in core academic areas, including reading, math, and science, when nature is included in the curriculum. Simply put, when the outdoors is included in a well-conceived program, learning increases and test scores reflect this." In addition, Kuo and Taylor (2005) found that "activities conducted in relatively natural outdoor settings were reported to reduce ADHD symptoms more than activities conducted in other settings" (p. 372). Overall, studies have shown that environment-based education can reduce discipline infractions, improve attendance, and bring to life subjects that are viewed by students as stale, boring, or irrelevant. See Figure 6.1 for a few examples of benefits of environment-based education from a compilation of research by Cheryl Charles, the president of the Children & Nature Network, and Alicia Senauer of Yale University (2010).

Figure 6.1 | **What Research Says About Nature Learning**

- **Play in natural settings helps develop a sense of self and indepen-dence.** A study by Lester and Maudsley (2006) indicates that "the power-ful combination of a diversity of play experiences and direct contact with nature has direct benefits for children's physical, mental, and emotional health" (pp. 4–5).

- **Schoolyard habitat projects bring natural benefits to schools and to students.** Rivkin (1997) observes that children have lost a connection to the outdoors due to such advancements as the automobile, yet they stand to gain much in terms of physical, cognitive, and emotional development by learning and playing outdoors.

- **Students' classroom behavior is better if they have recess.** A study by Barros, Silver, and Stein (2009) that analyzed data from more than 10,000 students in public and private schools found that teachers reported better classroom behavior from students who had recess. According to the study, "Recess may be an important element of classroom management and behavior guidance" (p. 435).

- **School gardens positively affect students' learning and behavior.** An in-depth research review by Blair (2009) notes that qualitative studies docu-ment a wide scope of benefits, including improved academic achievement, associated with learning experiences in school gardens. The author notes that "the teacher and principal are major variables in school-garden suc-cess" (p. 35).

In this world of increasing accountability and teacher burnout, nature learning can also provide educators with a fresh perspective on learning. According to Louv, "Canadian researchers found that teachers expressed renewed enthusiasm for teaching when they had time outdoors. In an era when teachers must do more with less, the impact of green schools and outdoor education on teachers' motivation should not be underestimated. Ultimately, K–12 education cannot be reformed without reforming higher education, which sets many of the standards and expectations for primary and secondary education. We'll need leaders who understand how the natural world works and how humans are a part of nature. Superintendents, principals, school board members—and teachers—are key elements."

Lighting the Learning Spark

I watched the upper-elementary class as it stood outside on a spring day. Students gathered around in small groups of four to look at leaves and comment on them. The students spoke excitedly while one member of each group took notes. Occasionally, a student would leave the huddle to retrieve another leaf from the nearby woods. The teacher went from group to group, listening and observing. Later in the day, the students would share their leaf samples on the live projector screen and discuss the various parts of the leaf and their functions.

Nearby, a preschool group walked alongside the edge of the woods on a stone dust trail while the teacher pointed out the different types of trees and brush. The 4- and 5-year-olds were unusually silent and attentive; their awe was palpable. As they looked and listened and felt the world around them, you could see the spark in their eyes.

Full disclosure: I am a former middle-grades science teacher. I love to learn outside, and I love to see students get outside and learn. I knew that students learned better when given real stimulus and the opportunity to experience nature with all their senses. When I think back to my "highlight reel" as a learner and as a teacher, I remember the following activities and how they lit that spark:

- As a middle school student, I went on a field trip to a colonial farm that was still powered by the force of water moving through a wheel.
- In college, my ecology professor encouraged us to closely examine the life found in hula-hoop-sized plots in the field behind our science center.
- As a second-year middle school science teacher, I took an 8th grade class spelunking through a limestone cave while we listened to our

guide explain the role of water in shaping the course of the narrow chambers.

- As principal, over the course of three school days, I took my entire school through a nature center that featured local flora and fauna, such as otters, turtles, and other wildlife. This experience broadened students' understanding and experience base. After we returned, the students shared their learning experiences through illustrations, discussions, and writing.

These learning experiences occurred outside the textbook, outside the computer lab, and outside the walls of the school building, and they helped learning come alive for students and adults alike. Today's leaders can expand the learning boundaries of their schools by enhancing students' awareness of the outdoors, catalyzing collaborative work among teachers, revitalizing school grounds, and enhancing school-community relations. We must get outside, and school leaders are uniquely poised to make an impact by focusing on learning outside the school.

Overcoming Challenges

Louv notes that "in recent years, too many school districts have turned classrooms inward, building windowless schools, banishing live animals from classrooms, and dropping recess and field trips." In times of budget shortfalls, there is often little funding or staffing to support massive outside projects. Yet as Louv points out, all of us can and should contribute to this work. By making nature learning a schoolwide focus for staff and by seeking support from the entire school community, this approach becomes more feasible. Here are some ways in which school leaders can overcome obstacles.

Apply for Grants for Resources

Opportunities abound for educators to seek grant funds for unique, outdoors-based learning initiatives. As an educator in Charlottesville, Virginia, I applied to the local Dave Matthews BAMA grant fund, which sought to benefit organizations that served at-risk students or focused on the protection of the environment. Making the case that today's students are at risk is not exactly a stretch: according to the Centers for Disease Control and Prevention, childhood obesity "continues to be a public health concern in the United States" (Ogden, Carroll, Curtin, Lamb, & Flegal, 2010, p. 242). Find local universities, charitable organizations, and grant opportunities that might be willing to fund, or match, efforts at your school to give children the opportunity to learn outdoors. For example, groups such as the Four Winds Nature Institute (www.fwni.org) have provided schoolyard mini-grants for projects that "enhance the schoolyard habitat by adding native plants and trees to attract birds, butterflies, or pollinators; building nature trails; or providing access to water (ponds or streams)" (Four Winds Nature Institute, 2011).

Involve Parents and Community Stakeholders

Louv notes that "schools can't do this alone—parents and whole communities must pitch in. Leaders should speak up for the kind of change they would like to see. New schools should be designed with nature in mind, and old schools retrofitted with playscapes that incorporate nature into the central design principle. Leaders can investigate the possibility of using nature preserves in an environment-based program, or the inclusion of established farms and ranches as part of 'new schoolyards.'" As principal, I worked with a lead teacher to solicit parent volunteers to help reshape and work with our "learning garden," which was named after a secretary who had worked at our school for 30 years. Parents and local community members signed up to spread mulch, plant bulbs, and remove weeds and brush. One parent who was a licensed massage therapist donated certificates for one-hour massage sessions to those who offered to build a compost bin (there were plenty of volunteers). There is no shortage of opportunities for innovation and unique learning opportunities when it comes to the outdoors.

Direct Attention to the Outdoors

Just by installing a few picnic tables to serve as both eating areas and learning centers, school leaders can emphasize the importance of being outdoors. By taking pictures of students and volunteers working outside and attaching a descriptive, grateful blurb on the school's website, a principal can draw attention to what is happening and infuse the community with a sense of wonder and appreciation. All too often, school pictures depict posed images of students tackling worksheets rather than digging their hands into fresh mulch or planting a group of tulip bulbs alongside the school walls. Whenever you are asked to do an interview, on any topic, pick an outdoor area that is significant to your learning community as the backdrop.

Action Items

As the research indicates, principals and teachers play a significant role in shaping nature learning for students. This is increasingly difficult in our test-driven climate, yet it is essential. By taking a few steps to infuse students' lives with the outdoors, principals and teachers can instill in students a sense of community and healthy priorities for years to come.

Create Ownership

Devote a faculty meeting to doing a "grounds walk" with your colleagues and discuss, first in small groups and then in a larger forum, ways in which your school might incorporate nature learning into existing curricular goals. Louv (2008) points out that "numerous studies document the benefits to students from school grounds that are ecologically diverse and include free-play areas, habitat for wildlife, walking trails, and gardens" (p. 219). Although school leaders may not have carte blanche to design, shape, and maintain the school grounds, they can create a strong sense of ownership from within by sharing ideas and discussing possibilities with the school community.

Enlist Volunteers

Enlist the help of parents and other volunteers, who can play a crucial role in the learning community by helping to weed nature learning areas, mulching during season changes, managing a compost pile, helping students (and teachers!) identify flora and fauna as a part of a learning project, trading services to local community members who can offer goods or services for grounds work, or performing summer upkeep and maintenance.

Highlight Your Nature Learning Initiatives

School leaders should make full use of their schools' websites, bulletin boards, community announcements and newsletters, and school improvement goals to highlight how learning can and does occur outside school walls. When I was a principal, I worked closely with our web designer to feature frequent clips of students learning in our learning garden, running outside on a new track, or composting waste. These clips demonstrated to the community the priority we placed on nature learning and celebrated the work that we were already doing.

Take Schoolwide Field Trips

Rather than just being grade-level rites of passage, field trips can serve two important purposes: to provide an opportunity to experience nature and to bring the learning community together. During the tenure of my principalship, I would work during the summer months to organize a schoolwide field trip in the fall that usually centered on nature learning. One year, we took all 300-plus students and more than 60 adults (including many parents) to a local cavern system, where we learned about the history and discovery of the cavern, explored its unique features, and experienced its cool, underground air and beautiful limestone formations. Our students and many of our parents and staff experienced a cavern for the first time and gained an appreciation for the natural world underground. By organizing the trip over the course of three consecutive days—we took two grade levels, or about 100 students, at a time—I was able to arrange for details such as costs and transportation and spread out the supervision responsibilities, which many of the teachers appreciated. Students brought back rich experiences, which bolstered their descriptive writing.

Provide Team Building for Staff

Ropes course, anyone? One summer, I worked with a local ropes course to organize a half-day team-building retreat for the teacher leaders in our school. Yes, this activity required a sense of humor and a willingness to sweat and combat the mosquitoes and sun, but we learned some valuable lessons on patience and teamwork and were reminded of our own affinity for the outdoors. Engaging in such activities helps leaders set an example for colleagues and reinforces that there is much to be learned from the outdoors.

Provide Team Building for Students

It is vitally important that students are positive leaders in their school communities. By participating in a "Nature Leadership Summit," teacher leaders, counselors, and administrators can instill values of trust and responsibility in their young leaders. Many local camps and recreational therapists offer ropes courses, team-building exercises, and other services that are tied in with nature learning.

Develop Thematic Units

Louv reminds us that "curriculum and standards need to be addressed. . . . In the forefront, of course, are budget concerns and the tripwires attached to testing standards." But by providing teams with planning time, a few parent volunteers, and a modest amount of funding to secure plants and other gardening items, school leaders can allow for living, breathing collaboration outdoors. For instance, why not begin teaching about the first Thanksgiving in spring by planting crops, with each grade level or subject area taking on a particular focus, and celebrating Thanksgiving, months later, as a school community? And Weilbacher (2009) describes a program at a Philadelphia middle school that engages students in outdoor field studies, including stream testing, canoeing, and trout rearing and release. In this program, students spend large blocks of time together outdoors and later build and use communication skills at conferences and youth summits.

Get Outdoors, Anytime, for Any Reason

You don't have to have a specific nature-based unit in place to benefit from the outdoors. An article in the Yuma, Arizona, newspaper *The Sun* describes a middle school language arts teacher who takes students outside to write poetry in an "improvised open-air classroom [that] prompted students to get in touch with feelings and rise to the challenge of inspired composition rather than just completing a written assignment" (Roller, 2009). Lawmakers in New Mexico recently secured funding to provide transportation to outdoor learning areas, such as state parks, to enable students to learn more about the outdoors and connect with nature (Gibbs, 2007). The bottom line is, students benefit individually and the classroom climate benefits as a whole from time spent in nature.

Let's Go Outside

If we want to change what happens within our school walls, perhaps we should start by learning outside them. Incorporating nature learning in our schools is necessary and revitalizing, and it can bring the community together. By seeking support and working toward deliberate goals, today's educators and leaders can address nature-deficit disorder in a variety of ways. Louv notes that nature learning is not limited to environmental science: "Recently, I've been most interested in the science teachers, English teachers, and many others who are not formally environmental educators, but do insist on taking their students outside to learn—to write poetry in a natural setting, for example, or to learn about science or history outdoors." Again, it is a challenge that all of us can and should accept: *Let's go outside and learn.*

In-the-Field Activities

1. At the beginning of a staff meeting, conduct a "nature walk audit" by walking the grounds as a department or staff and discussing the following:
   a. What areas are natural learning spaces for your students?
   b. What lessons have been successful in the past for other grade levels or subject areas, and how might you build on these in a vertical format to enhance your school's sense of community?
   c. What areas within your school's grounds might you improve to enhance learning? Consider practical ideas, such as installing benches in a shady area for reading groups, creating a trail alongside a tree line to allow for identification exercises, or setting up a water source or bird feeder to attract birds.
   d. Who are some community partners you might connect with to build and sustain nature learning in your school?

2. Louv believes that leaders and teachers should inform themselves about the cognitive and other health benefits of interacting with nature. He suggests researching such topics as "the benefits of unstructured free play, environment-based curricula, hands-on outdoor learning, and recess; the need for more natural schoolyard environments; the psychological benefits of natural settings; and nature's potential to reduce both stress and obesity" (personal communication, 2011). The Children & Nature Network website (www .childrenandnature.org) provides links to original research on these and other topics. Peruse and select one of these topics to consider and discuss as a team.

3. Plan a schoolwide field trip (in which you attend a location during a week as a school). Pick an area no more than a 45-minute bus trip away where you can learn about flora and fauna that are native to your area. While you plan the trip, consider the following questions:

   a. What grade levels should go at once, and what will the specific learning focus for each grade level be?
   b. What "common language" can you speak and discuss as a school during this week?
   c. How can you "share out" this experience with the entire school community?

4. Review the Action Items from this chapter and develop a plan to implement at least one in your school setting. How can the use of the outdoors enhance team building among both students and staff? Consider potential thematic units that would allow for vertical curricular collaboration among grade levels or departments. Consider seeking out grants and other external support to enhance nature learning. What steps are needed, and how will you communicate them to your team? What challenges do you anticipate? How will you reflect on your work after implementation?

Section 3

Challenges for Today

7

Turning Technology into Engaged Learning

I'm convinced that we administrative leaders have an obligation to initiate new learning, become skillful in the use of new tools that accelerate and advance our learning work, and share with others what we are learning.

—Pamela Moran

Action Items
* Develop critical thinking skills
* Affirm student and staff work
* Use technology to communicate
* Share meaningful data

Innovation in Instruction

Dr. Pamela Moran, the superintendent of Albemarle County Public Schools in Virginia, followed the principal into the upper-elementary classroom. The thuds of basketballs bouncing on a nearby court were easily heard through the classroom windows, but the outside activity went unnoticed by the students in the class, who gathered around tables covered with materials, laptops, and student sketches of designs. The students were engaged in an inquiry-based activity, using logarithms from laptop computers to direct robots to lift variously weighted objects over an obstacle on the floor. While Moran asked the students about the learning objective, the principal used a video camera to record the student responses and several trial runs where the robots successfully carried the objects or, in some cases, were bogged down by the weight, causing the students to rework their logarithms.

Moran, named one of the Top 10 Tech-Savvy Superintendents by *eSchool News* in 2010 for "exemplifying outstanding leadership in the use of technology to further educational goals" (Devaney, 2010), promotes hands-on, student-focused learning in the 26 diverse schools in her division. Despite budget setbacks and rising accountability benchmarks, Moran has led the school division through a variety of innovative changes. In an age when superintendents are being increasingly inundated with various crises, Moran has strategically planned for technology infusion throughout every facet of the division. As one of Moran's principals, I was fortunate to take part in numerous projects like the inquiry-based activity described above.

From supporting virtual e-resource innovations and 1:1 computing projects to putting iPhones in the hands of principals to enable them to capture live data during learning walks, Moran has committed to improving the educational experience of each student by equipping schools with technologies that save time, enhance universal access to crucial information, showcase successes of various stakeholders, and align system work in a productive manner. This kind of approach takes deliberate, reflective effort on the part of the leader. As Brooks-Young (2009) notes, "Many school administrators now have the latest, greatest gadgets in the office or on campus, and they have not made a bit of difference in students' academic achievement. What does make a difference is a school administrator at any level who is a thoughtful instructional leader" (p. 16). Moran insists that

> educating our young people well is a matter of America's national security and economic future. We have no time to waste and no children to waste. We cannot wait on the federal or state government to figure out what we educators already know. Our young people need learning spaces that may be on a school bus, in a classroom, in a coffee shop, at the local library, or in their homes. They need universal access to experts and information that can be available anytime and anywhere. They need teachers who intersect content with pedagogical and technological expertise and who continue to evolve as career learners themselves. We need to set learning expectations against international benchmarks and college and workforce readiness skills, much of which can only be measured through performance assessments, not selected-response test items.

Moran and other tech-savvy leaders believe it is vital to help our students and staffs use technology effectively—not for technology's sake but for *learning's* sake.

Leading and Learning Through Technology

Moran embraces current trends in technology to enhance leadership and further student learning. She believes that the onus is on the educational leader not only to be aware of new technologies but also to serve as an innovative leader in the field by introducing and modeling these technologies and continually leading by example. "In my superintendent world," she notes, "I work to learn, choose, and use innovating technologies that will help me communicate more effectively. I work to model choices of technology that allow us to accomplish work we otherwise could not do as efficiently and effectively. And I know that if I can't stay current then I will not be able to get my colleagues to do the same."

Moran leads by example. From maintaining a blog to equipping schools with iPads, iPods, and Activeboards and all division buses with the latest GPS hardware, Moran has stood out as a technology leader in the education field.

She defines technology leadership as "creating learning spaces, some individual and some collaborative, in order to fulfill both horizontal and vertical learning directions."

Leading experts in the field agree with Moran's philosophy, promoting a proactive, involved approach to technology that is centered on both action and reflection. Brooks-Young (2009), on behalf of the International Society for Technology in Education, writes that educational leaders should "facilitate the shared development by all stakeholders of a vision for technology use and widely communicate that vision" (p. 17). For instance, a principal could lead a faculty meeting on engagement by conducting a primary math counting competition using SMART Boards in which teachers showcase their own problem-solving strategies and work together in teams. By formulating a vision that is steeped in a reflective understanding of the organization's current and desired states and by modeling and integrating technology in a systematic way, the leader can serve as a tech-savvy example to the community.

One crucial component of technology leadership is *shared* leadership. The leader alone cannot effectively infuse technology into an organization. Davies (2010) explains the problem with the all-too-common top-down approach to technology leadership:

> The associations between educational technology leadership and school change are yet to be addressed directly. What exists is prescriptive, rather than descriptive, and conceptual. On the whole there is a dominance of elite adults. . . . Teachers and students are key underpinning considerations for technology leadership, but these voices are missing from the literature. (p. 59)

Moran has worked tirelessly to supply staff—from teachers to bus drivers, instructional coaches, and principals—with the tools and impetus to use technology within their respective arenas. She also equips teacher leaders to conduct workshops on how to use such applications as SMART Boards, video cameras, or Prezi (cloud-based presentation software), and encourages principals to show their entire staffs how to infuse technology into the learning process.

"Back to the Future" with Shared Human Communication

Have you ever considered that in this age of increasing technological advances, we might actually be traveling back in time with regard to how we communicate as humans? Moran, who has served as an educator for more than 30 years in such capacities as high school biology teacher, teacher leader, principal, and superintendent, notes that the advent of recent technological advances has truly accelerated change in the field of education: "The advances that we have had in these past few years have allowed us to almost return to a pre–Gutenberg era in which we now communicate and learn again through the oral traditions of early storytellers." We can post a YouTube clip of a Shakespeare play, tweet an excerpt from a commencement address, and Skype an important message to our family. Recent headlines confirm this trend: in a recent Associated Press article titled "Wear wristwatch? Use e-mail? Not for Class of '14," Ramde (2010) describes a study that confirmed that not only do students seldom use "snail mail," but they also rely much less on written communication in general, preferring to use verbal and visual modes.

Moran is influenced by the perspectives of Ira David Socol, author of the SpeEdChange blog (http://speedchange.blogspot.com), who articulates this trend in a short presentation titled "Human Communication" (2010; available for viewing at www.youtube.com/watch?v=7UXh7Vb1XL8). In this presentation, he describes how the practice of telling stories and working with adaptive texts and modes of communication is returning educators to pre–Gutenberg approaches, and he declares that the current era of fixed text is ending. Socol believes that we are moving from linear, concrete text to a new, unfixed mode that allows us to categorize, process, engage with, and share information in a different way. Socol's "open notion of authorship" (personal communication, 2010) empowers the technology user and innovator to use "high–Bloom's taxonomy" tools, such as creativity, application, and evaluation, rather than relying solely on lower-order cognitive skills such as memorization and comprehension.

Overcoming Challenges

Implementing technology in ways that are feasible, productive, student-focused, and relevant can be difficult. Often, leaders lean heavily on a technology liaison or even an outside consultant to bolster their technology credibility. Here are some ways in which leaders can take ownership of technological innovation in their schools.

Take Risks, Take Criticisms, and Persist in Innovating

In her various roles as teacher, principal, assistant superintendent for student learning, and now superintendent of schools, Moran has encountered numerous barriers to effectively integrating technology. For example, the local newspaper published editorials complaining about her use of a handheld iPhone during graduation ceremonies. She reflects, "I never was criticized when I had my Canon 250 camera and a pad of paper to capture images and speech content from graduations in the past, but my doing the same thing in an instant Twitter format gave some of our parents pause." Being innovative is not always appreciated or understood, and Moran admits that change is not always easy. Still, she took the complaints in stride and continues to seek out innovation.

Moran acknowledges that taking the lead on using new technologies can also challenge her own learning capabilities. In a blog post, she reflects that "becoming an educator with the contemporary knowledge and skills to influence and teach others is as essential an expectation of administrative leaders as it is for teachers. Our kids don't wait around on someone to tell them to learn a new technology and neither should we. It's why I push myself to use tools that are alien in my hands today" (Moran, 2010b).

Embed Resources in Collaborative Staff Time

Another challenge to integrating technology is finding adequate time and an appropriate manner to share the applications with colleagues in the field. As Moran notes, "You can have all the resources in the world, but if they are sitting there unused, then they are not effectively moving the organization, or learning, forward." November (2010) believes that "the real bottleneck to the creative use of technology is staff development. There are too many exciting technologies—web design, digital video editing, presentation tools, probes, content-specific tools—and not enough time for teachers to learn them" (p. 48).

I have found that when division leaders, principals, and team or department leaders use time already set aside for collaborative efforts to showcase a new lesson or application, colleagues take notice in a positive way. For example, a math team leader might share a new math application that requires an imaging projector by bringing the projector and manipulatives to a faculty meeting and demonstrating setup, coordination of materials, and overall use of the equipment. Seeing a colleague use something in an effective and relevant manner makes the "next big thing" seem more feasible.

Reflect and Recharge

Today's school leaders function at an increasingly hurried pace. Mike Connolly (2007) observes that "far from being the models of self-control, balance, and rationality they should be, many principals resemble butterflies on speed pills; they can't devote sustained attention to anything" (p. 32). Pam Moran emphasizes that in our fast-paced "iPod world," in which we are constantly inundated with information and stimulation, we need to value solitude and quiet. Moran finds that contributing to blogs such as Edurati Review (http://eduratireview.com) and her own blog, A Space for Learning (http://spacesfor learning.wordpress.com), is a good way to reflect on her practice. By articulating her thoughts in posts that draw on her experiences and refer to her vision, she is able to model the importance of reflection and meaningful conversation for the greater professional learning community. Moran is "concerned that the art of sustained dialogue is being lost in a world in which we often engage in sound-bite information exchange—whether it is print media or face-to-face conversation. The 'hurried child' has become the 'hurried adult'—I fear—to the detriment of deep learning."

Action Items

Technology cannot be discussed in the abstract; educators must make it work for themselves and for their students in a meaningful, tangible way. New technology cannot sit unopened on a bookshelf or uninstalled on a computer and be effective. It must be explored, implemented, and shared with a purpose to enhance and improve learning. The use of technology in schools can serve as a catalyst for engaged learning, teamwork, affirmation, and student achievement.

Develop Critical Thinking Skills

Although educators may ceaselessly debate among themselves such topics as the merits of cursive handwriting and the correct approach to teaching math and reading, they agree pretty unanimously on the need for students to acquire critical thinking skills. Used wisely, technology can be a useful aid in promoting these skills. November (2010) believes that teachers should use technology to "provide structure and direction to a student's ability to make meaning" (p. 72). For example, by having a student use a SMART Board in front of the class to predict the next shape in a pattern, a 1st grade teacher allows the student to model critical thinking skills for the class. Leaders can use technology to this end, too. Moran encourages her principals to connect with their school communities via Prezi visual presentation. By modeling a Prezi or a handheld observation application to her principals in a monthly meeting, she shows the nuts and bolts involved in implementing technology in a relevant manner. Students and staff alike benefit from practical application of new technologies and hone their thinking skills as they evaluate, synthesize, and apply these skills and processes in their learning and in their work.

Affirm Student and Staff Work

As principal, I was able to affirm students' and staff members' work in real time by posting video clips to the opening of a faculty meeting taken from within the walls of the school building. As Moran actively tours her 26 schools, she, too, shares images and work samples that provide collaborative insights from the division that can help teachers and principals synthesize learning that is occurring in other schools and adapt it to their own learning environments.

This affirmative approach not only disseminates best practices and updates the community on schools' doings, but also bolsters morale. Moran routinely affirms staff on Twitter (www.twitter.com/pammoran). For example, on the opening workday of 2010, Moran tweeted the following message: "All #acps teachers return today—a gift to our learners who benefit from their dedication, care, & the sacrifices they make simply 2 teach" (Moran, 2010a). The teachers who follow Moran on Twitter were aware that she was thinking of their return and affirming their collective efforts.

In an age when principals and teacher leaders are conducting ever shorter walk-through observations, technology can facilitate an authentic and dynamic exchange of ideas. Many walk-through data systems incorporate a handheld component that enables the observer to immediately share with the classroom teacher his or her observations on student engagement, student articulation of the learning objective, and high-yield strategies used. As principal, I encouraged my teachers to reply to my observations, and they often took me up on that offer. At times, they disagreed with my notes, which was fine with me. The important thing was to continue the dialogue.

Use Technology to Communicate

Today's technologies enable educational leaders to instantly reach their communities with precision and clarity. Once, during a weekend trip, I was notified of a tragedy that had befallen our school community, and I was able to use my iPhone and laptop as a communication outreach system to craft a message to send to our communications director for approval; activate a phone tree for our staff to follow our crisis manual procedures; and upload the approved message through a portal to synchronously arrive at parents' designated phone numbers. As principal, I used this carefully maintained communication system to reach the school community about everything from flu shots and Bingo Night to such time-sensitive issues as a suspected gas leak.

Communication technologies like Skype also allow educators to go "back to the future" with old-fashioned interaction with other classrooms, educators, and presenters, despite being miles apart. I have used a laptop to communicate with panels of educators many states away to debate a hot topic, share a collaborative idea via Prezi, or tell a story. Such real-time interaction boosts engagement and learning.

Share Meaningful Data

Moran's team uses Keynote and Prezi technologies to share student achievement data and emphasize key points related to instruction and learning. Whereas reams of Excel spreadsheets may intimidate even the most mathematically inclined school community member, crystallized interactive charts depicting shrinking achievement gaps speak volumes to the work of the organization. The division's motto, "All Means All," requires the work of the staff to meet the needs of all students. By ensuring that these data have meaning—particularly with regard to students and targeted achievement areas—Moran can align the efforts of the staff in prioritizing continued growth. For example, Moran's school district uses a centralized online server to consolidate data and curriculum. Although, Moran concedes, the work was "messy" for the first few years, as teachers and administrators learned to navigate through the new software, it has continually improved the accessibility of the data and the curriculum and fostered understanding and collaboration in the learning community. Teachers are able to look at student achievement data in the database by a particular area, or strand, with a few clicks of the mouse.

The Active, Innovative Leader

"You can be a leader anywhere if you are active on the social media stage," Moran declares. Today's educational leaders are ideally positioned to analyze, disseminate, and respond to critical information—and they should not rely on subordinates or colleagues to do this work. Moran strongly advocates leading by example; as she (2010b) points out, "Why would we expect more from teacher colleagues and young learners than from ourselves?"

Moran draws on her experience and training as a high school science teacher in defining what she calls her "EcoEdusystem"—that is, her frame of reference for "how all the bits of education come together and allow us to leverage incredible talents, dispositions, and skills" (personal communication, 2010). Here's how she describes her inspiration for this EcoEdusystem:

> Often, the natural world is the source of metaphorical perspective for me in making sense of new information, ideas, or skills. It's the spicebush and tiger swallowtails, viceroys and skippers gathered on Russian thistles that remind me of how people crowd-source together as diverse communities in which they come together for common purposes, share common dreams, and engage in common behaviors despite their differences. (personal communication, 2010)

Moran is able to enhance the strengths of individuals and of her school division as a whole by using technology in a full, robust manner that allows for shared ownership of student success. By engaging the entire school community and appreciating its diversity, Moran is able to realize its "common purposes" in a way that often eludes educational organizations.

In-the-Field Activities

1. Attend a class, seminar, board meeting, or faculty meeting and note any technologies you see being used. If you do not observe any, suggest ways in which a faculty meeting could use technology to
   a. Showcase student work;
   b. Provide examples of collaboration;
   c. Highlight, in a succinct manner, updates on achieving organizational goals or objectives; or
   d. Share other ideas to enhance school community work.

2. What technology might enable you to engage your colleagues in a way that encourages them to use the same technology in their own work?

3. Consider how you currently use technology. Create an action plan to integrate one new approach that will help you reach your school community more effectively. How will you know if you are successful?

4. Review the Action Items from this chapter and develop a plan to implement at least one in your school setting. Consider using an innovative shared "human communication," such as YouTube, Twitter, or Skype, to connect with another educator in the field. How can using technology in your position as a leader enhance your own critical thinking skills and your students'? Consider changing the way you affirm students and staff in your learning community. What steps are needed, and how will you communicate them to your team? What challenges do you anticipate? How will you reflect on your work after implementation?

8

Turning Data into Action

Is an adjustment needed, and, if so, what should that adjustment be?

—*James Popham*

Action Items
* Share results
* Create an organized framework
* Provide feedback to students
* Align resources with the big picture

Assess, Adjust, Act

Educator and researcher James Popham has taught for more than three decades at both the secondary and the university level, principally at the University of California, Los Angeles. He has researched and written extensively about assessment—most notably, formative assessment—and has worked with numerous schools and organizations to help principals and teacher leaders in this important work.

In his book *Transformative Assessment* (2008), Popham contends that we cannot afford to wait until quarter or semester breaks to dig into the data, but that we must assess students routinely and often. Teachers and principals need to be engaged in the process and ready to *adjust* in response to the data. Popham asserts that educators' "decisions to adjust or not adjust, and the decisions about the nature of any adjustments . . . need to be made on the spot or almost on the spot—when there's still instructional and learning time available" (p. 11). Constant reflection and a willingness to change course are essential in formative assessment. Teachers must be open to making changes in their approaches and to helping students recognize that they may need to make changes of their own.

According to Fisher and Frey (2007), "The act of checking for understanding not only corrects misconceptions; it can also improve learning" (p. 2). By transforming data into action, educators follow students' growth, not a dusty lesson plan.

Data: Do They Mean Anything?

It was early July, and I was starting at my new school as the third principal in three years. I sorted through the detritus left behind by the last few principals. I found old T-shirt samples with the school logo and previous years' School Improvement Plan files. Then I came to a row of bulging binders neatly placed on the top shelf of the storage closet. They stood out prominently because they were marked by year and lined up in chronological order. Each binder was labeled with the same big block letters: DATA. I picked up a binder and thumbed through it, and my eyes immediately glazed over. I was suddenly a 3rd grader again, trying to read sheet music during my piano lesson. I wondered, "What is the importance of these data? Do they make a difference in the way we do things? Does this really mean anything to anyone?"

We live and work in an age of high-stakes accountability. Parents browsing real-estate guides often Google a neighborhood school's data to get a sense of whether or not the school is a "good school." Teachers are evaluated on data. Principals are fired because of data. And schools are labeled because of data.

So the answer is yes: like it or not, data *do* matter. But that doesn't mean that all data are created equal. As principal, I wanted to know what students were learning, how teachers were guiding their learning, and what I could do to encourage their efforts. But I did not want to wait until the summer returns to know how our students were doing.

Summative Versus Formative Assessment

Summative assessment data is often called "autopsy data" by researchers, because it is taken after the fact and doesn't serve "patients," or students, at the time when they really need the help. Summative assessments are often developed by a testing service or by committee members at the state department of education level. In contrast, formative assessment is interactive and is shaped by teachers and, ideally, students. Popham (2008) sees formative assessment as "a potentially transformative instructional tool" (p. 3) that can benefit both educators and students. Figure 8.1 provides a general overview of formative and summative assessment.

According to Popham (2010), the key to good assessment isn't whether it's formative or summative, but whether teachers and students use "assessment evidence to make adjustments in what they're doing" (p. 4). When I was a principal, I tended to define formative assessment as something that we had control over at the school level, whereas summative assessment was something that was mandated and already in place, with little room for adjustment.

Figure 8.1 | **Formative Versus Summative Assessments**

Type of assessment	Formative	Summative
When given?	During learning.	After learning.
Examples	Exit slips, prompts, interviews, demonstrations, quick response, discussion participation.	Multiple-choice "bubble test," essay or written response, independent simulation or demonstration.
Characterization	Can be "messy," jotted down, given verbally, differentiated, informal.	Usually neat, clean, consistent, "scannable," formal.
Roles	Teacher and learner as active participants and change agents.	Teacher (or state) as evaluator, learner as subject of evaluation.
Importance	Helps determine next steps for teacher and student to facilitate learning.	Determines pass or fail status, end grade, or other designation.
Advice for principals and teacher leaders	Use for insight into student learning, adjustments, grouping, pacing, and collaboration.	Use to highlight key strands (for growth areas and targets) and for overall perspective on students.

Source: From *Checking for Understanding: Formative Assessment Techniques for Your Classroom* (p. 4), by D. Fisher and N. Frey, 2007, Alexandria, VA: ASCD. © 2007 by ASCD.

The Importance of Formative Assessment

Popham explained to me that although formative assessment "helps students learn better," it may not improve outcomes on "the wrong kinds of accountability tests" (i.e., the high-stakes assessments that vary from state to state). However, if formative assessment consistently demonstrates growth both for individual students and for the class as a whole, then students are indeed learning.

Popham insists that today's school leaders "must understand the formative assessment process." And once school leaders understand the process, they "must ensure that teachers do it; if you can just get teachers to do the formative assessment, the behavior shifts the attitudes in support of using formative assessment." Student buy-in is also essential. Popham strongly advocates helping students use formative assessment to monitor their own learning and allowing them to make some decisions during the learning process. In a 4th grade math classroom, for example, the teacher might give students extra time to spend at a learning station using manipulatives without explicit instructions to simply maintain their engagement in the tools and help them gain number sense. A high school Spanish teacher could give students a choice to practice verb conjugation through dialogue with a peer or to work alone at a more routine vocabulary memorization module, depending on students' current comfort level.

The Formative Assessment Cycle

Formative assessment is meant to allow for reflection as well as purposeful action, so it requires the perspective of the PLC as well as of the individual teacher. Ideally, the whole approach should look like this:

1. Teachers meet as a team to discuss learning objectives and create authentic assessments that allow for reflection and change.

2. Teachers engage students in lessons while using the assessments to check on the students' learning along the way.

3. Teachers meet again to discuss the assessment data and their implications and to decide on necessary changes and next steps.

4. The planning, teaching, assessment, and analysis process begins all over again.

I call this process the Data into Action Cycle (see Figure 8.2).

Implementing Schoolwide Formative Assessments

As Popham notes, implementing a new schoolwide (or departmentwide) process of formative assessment can be difficult. He advocates forming a

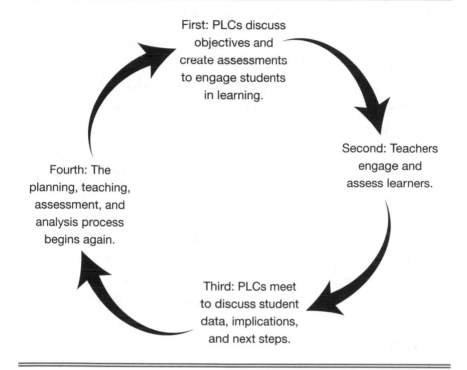

Figure 8.2 | **Data into Action Cycle**

First: PLCs discuss objectives and create assessments to engage students in learning.

Second: Teachers engage and assess learners.

Third: PLCs meet to discuss student data, implications, and next steps.

Fourth: The planning, teaching, assessment, and analysis process begins again.

systematic plan to strengthen the school community's understanding of the formative assessment process. This introductory plan should include the following steps.

Step 1: Understand and Explain the Formative Assessment Process

Formative assessment is not just tests and quizzes; it's a planned process. Popham says that the deliberateness of the process is sometimes distorted by principals who think formative assessment consists of "giving an occasional interim test." Formal training, in the context of school staff development, is essential to ensure consistency, clarity, and productive team discussion. In

Transformative Assessment, Popham offers several key points (see the following bulleted list) that educators should keep in mind when considering formative assessment:

- **Learning progression.** A learning progression consists of "step-by-step building blocks" that students must go through to "successfully attain a more distant, designated instructional outcome" (Popham, 2008, p. 24). For instance, PLC teams might work together to help students learn how to take complex data sets and convert them into meaningful charts and tables.

- **Enabling knowledge.** *Enabling knowledge* is low-Bloom's material that the student must memorize to move on in the learning process. Just as in building a learning progression, educators must be deliberate in setting learning goals to build the right foundation blocks for students.

- **Subskills.** A subskill is a cognitive skill that students must attain before moving on. For example, Popham (2008) points out that subskills necessary for writing an essay would be the abilities "to (1) properly organize the essay's content and (2) create an attention-arresting opening paragraph" (p. 25).

Step 2: Get Teacher Buy-In by Sharing Relevant Research

Popham, citing Wiliam (2007), says, "If you do formative assessment well, you can essentially double the speed of student learning." He suggests that teachers "start small" by using formative assessment once a week, and then increase the use. By showing concrete examples of how this process has worked in similar grade levels or subject areas, the educational leader can foster a can-do attitude among staff. Fisher and Frey's (2007) *Checking for Understanding: Formative Assessment Techniques for Your Classroom* emphasizes that assessment should serve and lead into better learning, and the authors provide examples and strategies across the grade levels and content areas. Rose, Minton, and Arline (2007) provide concrete examples of formative assessment probes in their book *Uncovering Student Thinking in Mathematics.* Popham has also written a book titled *Transformative Assessment in Action: An Inside Look at Applying the Process,* in which he provides a framework for educators to think through and apply the process in their schools. In addition, the leader should closely follow journals in curriculum and instruction or educational leadership, which often provide relevant and timely resources from the field.

Step 3: Discuss the Different Types of Formative Assessment

Popham emphasizes the importance of spending time discussing, as grade- or subject-level teams, the various "levels," or functions, of formative assessment, which are "fundamentally distinguishable from each other" (2008, p. ix):

Level 1: Teacher adjustments. Teachers collect evidence that they use to adjust their current and future instruction.

Level 2: Student adjustments. Students use formative assessment to make their own adjustments in learning strategies.

Level 3: Classroom climate. A classroom-level shift occurs: instead of using assessment to compare students with one another, teachers and students use it to focus on what they can do to improve learning.

Level 4: Schoolwide implementation. The entire school adopts formative assessment in professional development and teacher learning communities.

Recognizing that incorporating formative assessment practices can be a significant shift, Popham (2008) cautions educators not to "let pursuit of the instructionally perfect prevent you from reaping the rewards of the instructionally possible" (p. ix).

Overcoming Challenges

Both students and teachers play a vital role in the ongoing, interactive formative assessment process. As with any implementation of a major new approach, there will be obstacles. Here are some ways to address challenges that commonly crop up.

Overcome Entrenched Behaviors

Selling a new assessment approach to a group of educators can be daunting. As Popham reminds us, "We are dealing with human beings who have been successful in teaching. You are asking them to modify a set of behaviors that have served them very well."

To overcome entrenchment, you need to show how the change is going to be better, in the long run, for both the teachers and students involved. You might explain to the staff, for example, that a new approach in using formative assessment will be coupled with additional planning time that will enable staff to authentically discuss, and prepare for, student achievement. It is also a good idea to take something else off the table—for example, assessments that align more with the summative approach, like biweekly bubble tests.

Use Standardized-Test Data for Good

The hopeful teacher, principal, or division leader may be disillusioned if he or she is looking for a quick initial bump in achievement on standardized tests. Classroom assessments are a measure of what happens in the classroom. Depending on your state's test, the teaching and learning in your classrooms may not be aligned with the state bubble test. Acknowledging and addressing this disconnect is a conversation worth having at both the division and the school level. But it is important not to be dismissive of standardized tests, telling a school board or colleagues, "Forget the state test, our kids are learning." No. Data speak: the newspapers will show data, and they will likely be about the state test. This is the world we live in; high-stakes tests matter. But *student learning* matters more, and any work that we do should be open, accessible, and usable. My advice? Be transparent about the data. They are what they are, and they do provide a picture of the school's current state. Showing student, cohort, and grade-level data can be helpful in showing growth, focus areas, and next steps. And chances are, with greater collaborative discussion, analysis of results, discussion on next steps, and a focus on student engagement and input, progress on high-stakes tests will be realized over time.

Foster Active Teamwork

As obvious as it sounds, it's worth emphasizing that working in teams requires active teamwork. A grade-level or department team must not rely on just one of its members to create and disseminate assessments, because formative assessment is an interactive process that should involve all teachers and students as they progress through the learning goals. An imbalance of effort deteriorates the ownership of this work. The most effective teams I have known examine the curriculum together, plan and agree on all assessments before sharing them with learners, and then discuss assessment results collectively. Students should be treated and discussed as individuals, and this takes time. By mutually owning this important work, teachers share challenges and successes alike while strengthening all students' learning in a manner that is both effective and efficient.

Action Items

As principal, I realized that I had to put a few important components in place if I wanted to foster effective assessment in our school. The reality today is that school leaders will have to grapple with summative assessment, such as high-stakes end-of-grade tests, as well as formative assessment. Both formative and summative assessment can benefit the school's understanding of student achievement in a practical way. The role of the leader is to work out the details and to set priorities in using the data effectively.

Share Results

Even if a school or a department is a well-oiled machine, it may grapple with examining and presenting data, particularly in formal meetings such as a Quarterly Review, in which a school presents data to members of the school staff as well as the division, or a School Improvement Team planning session, which is geared more exclusively to the school. Here's what to focus on:

1. **Share your process.** Provide an overview of your team's approach and emphasize students' learning gains.

2. **Highlight goals.** Discuss important areas of growth, making sure to tie them in with the school or division goals.

3. **Show progress.** Discuss specific progress that is being made by groups of students (e.g., by grade level, demographic group, or specific class) and in particular grade- or subject-level strands (e.g., measurement and geometry in a 4th grade math class). Showing a year-by-year comparison of both formative and summative assessment data can be helpful. Be sure to incorporate occasional anecdotes of particular students' success.

4. **Describe next steps.** As Figure 8.2 illustrates, the formative assessment process is never done. By discussing next steps and expected outcomes on future assessments, teachers can keep the focus on continual improvement for students and staff alike.

Create an Organized Framework

Teachers must know what they are expecting their students to learn. They should start by looking at existing data by particular subject strand so that they get a current-state perspective of where the school (or department) stands. This perspective is aligned with DuFour's four crucial questions to guide the work of educators (What do we want each student to learn? How will we know when each student has learned it? How will we respond when a student experiences difficulty in learning? How will we respond when a student is proficient?).

As a principal, I worked with our elementary math specialist to devise goals for using exit slips (Sterrett & Fiddner, 2007) that included one question aligned to the learning objective in that particular math class. They were not solely a bubble-choice or test-preparation format, and they provided an opportunity for students to demonstrate problem solving in a specific area.

We wanted teams to be able to look at data in a regular, authentic manner, so we set a goal for two exit slips per week. Twice a week, at the end of the lesson, teachers would hand out a math problem and, after receiving students' answers, indicate on a roster chart whether or not each student had mastered a certain understanding or skill.

Figure 8.3 | **Sample Exit Slip Roster**

	Objective 3.1: Compare and order (clicker response)	Objective 3.1: Place value, problem 1 (manipulatives)	Objective 3.1: Place value, problem 2 (sentence explanation)	Objective 3.2: Estimating sums and differences (multiple-choice)	Objective 3.3: Estimating quotients (sentence explanation)
Amy	x	√	x	√	√
Angel	√	√	√	√	√
Guillermo	√	x	√	√	√
	Strand: *Number and Number Sense*				Strand: *Multiplication and Division*

Source: From "Snapshot Portraits of Math Achievement: The Vital Role of Math Exit Slips in the Elementary Setting," by W. Sterrett and P. Fiddner, 2007, *Virginia Educational Leadership, 5*(1), pp. 94–97. © 2007 by Virginia ASCD. Adapted with permission.

Over time, those two exit slips per week enabled teams to better understand how individual students were doing and how different cohorts or classes were performing. Organized over time, the exit slips also provided a snapshot portrait of student success by strand (see Figure 8.3). Exit slip results were organized into a simple roster with a "correct" or "incorrect" notation next to each strand or objective tested. These rosters could be turned in weekly or biweekly, with the sample problems attached. This strategy showed teachers which strands demanded more attention, whether that meant they needed to regroup students, deepen or extend their instruction, use more-targeted materials for the particular strand, or engage in professional growth activities.

Provide Feedback to Students

Effective formative assessment allows for adjustments to be made. It also provides teachers with the opportunity to give valuable feedback to students and help them monitor their own progress. According to Popham, teachers "have to be willing to back away from the notion that you have to make the decision as a teacher, and instead give the student the opportunity to move in a certain direction" and take responsibility for their learning. This will lead teachers to, again, make adjustments in their instruction by prioritizing time to provide feedback—and to listen—to students. The teacher must find time to meet with students individually to help them understand how they are performing and where they need to go, and to discuss ways in which they can meet their goals.

Align Resources with the Big Picture

Building leaders are in charge of resources; it's that simple. Thus, principals and team leaders should work together to monitor overall team progress as well as, when possible, individual cohort and student progress to ensure that the school is realizing continual progress in a systematic manner. All too often, the squeaky wheel (or team member) gets the resources, such as teacher assistant time or additional funds for supplies. But resources should be distributed systematically, with an eye on the big picture. Thus, rather than be *reactive* and hastily move people and schedules around in response to perceived needs, the principal needs to be *proactive* and consider the learning organization as a whole. The leader should, at least quarterly, review the data with an external reviewer (such as a liaison at the central-office level or even a principal colleague from another school) to ensure that the school's approach is working toward overall progress rather than focusing on one particular area to the detriment of others.

Giving Life to the Data

Learning is complicated. Assessing learning can be even more complicated. By giving life to those binders of data, those reams of analyses, and those student report cards, the entire learning community can share a stake in what matters most: student growth. This process requires time, clarity, and honesty about next steps. But translating data into action by integrating meaningful classroom assessments that allow for flexibility, student voice, and collaborative change will enable today's learning communities to realize the benefits of improved student learning and professional collaboration.

In-the-Field Activities

1. Choose a particular learning target from a strand of a subject area that you teach (or have taught or would like to teach). What kind of formative assessment would be appropriate for your learners? Share your thoughts with a partner and discuss your approaches as a grade- or subject-level team.

2. Find a team or department that has a reputation for being highly functional. Coordinate a visit to its next team meeting and ask team members how they approach assessment and collaborate on this work.

3. Arrange to observe a colleague's class and offer to design an effective exit slip for him or her to use the next day as he or she opens class. What important components will you consider as you create the exit slip? How might this approach affect your colleague's teaching?

4. Review the Action Items from this chapter and develop a plan to implement at least one in your school setting. How can you implement a Data into Action Cycle in your school or team? What would it look like? What might an organized framework for exit slips look like for a middle school math team, and what clear expectations would be important to consider? How about for a high school biology team? As you consider the role of collaborative, action-oriented assessment work, consider what steps are needed and how you will communicate them to your team. What challenges do you anticipate? How will you reflect on your work after implementation?

Turning Today's Challenges into Success

A crisis allows you to take initiative and capture the knowledge, the skills, the attitude, and the human capital to create something new that helps solve persistent problems. All you need is persistence and confidence.

—Yvonne Chan

Action Items
* Develop a crisis plan
* Align the organization
* Prioritize personal health
* Find success partners
* Learn to triage

"From Crack House to Schoolhouse"

Principal Yvonne Chan embodies success. Having transformed a poverty-ridden public school into the first charter school in Los Angeles and the first conversion charter school in the United States, Dr. Chan has overseen considerable change in her school community. By transcending her role as principal and providing the community with services in health care, nutrition, and family social services, she has successfully redefined her role and fostered change in the community. Along the way, she has realized personal success as well, receiving the Milken National Educator Award in 1991, the Blue Ribbon of Distinction in 1996, and the Gleitsman Foundation Citizen Activist Award in 2004. She has also served on local, statewide, and national panels and commissions focused on student success and overcoming poverty.

Yet throughout her journey, she has encountered tremendous challenges. Some, such as student deaths, made a lasting impact on her. Others, such as colleague dissension and jealousy, she took in stride. When I asked Chan what was involved in moving an organization from good to great, she emphasized that overcoming challenges is essential in moving forward, even when there are setbacks along the way.

In 1993, Chan was considered a rising star in the Los Angeles Unified School Division. As a female minority immigrant who spoke Spanish and had a doctorate from the University of California, Los Angeles, she was in high demand and "could write my own ticket," she notes. She began as a teacher in the division in 1968 and worked her way up through the ranks, eventually serving as principal. She was assigned to the Vaughn School in 1990 following racial conflict there and even a death threat to the previous principal. When she arrived, many of her teachers had "emergency credentials," and others were literally counting down the minutes to retirement. She spent much of her time working to increase safety, organize details such as bus routes, revitalize instructional focus, and turn around the school. Yet her heart continued to focus her work on students who reminded her of her own background, coming to the United States as a young girl living in poverty. Scores stayed persistently low despite her efforts and some measure of improvement. Recognizing Vaughn's need for stability, she chose to stay and lead her school into a new direction as the first charter school in Los Angeles.

Overcoming Challenges

The role of the school leader is not simply to give a high-five to a student who beat the odds and passed, or to wave farewell to buses at the end of a great school year filled with wonderful memories, or to walk down a neatly polished hallway awaiting the first day of school with an excited mix of emotions. It's all of that but so much more, and if we are not careful, the "more" can overwhelm us. Chan advises leaders not to "label these happenings as crises" but "as opportunities." Let us envision a sampling of the challenges and opportunities that today's school leaders face.

Resolve Crises, Transform the School

Chan describes the tragic loss of three students over a two-year span in the early 1990s, during her early years as principal at the inner-city Vaughn Learning Center: "The immediate reaction was to raise money to bury the kids. But at that very moment, I was determined that there must be a health clinic on site. Not just for the kids, but for the entire school community." Chan forged ahead and led this effort; she developed her plan to build a clinic on site and incorporate it into the school, when the charter school movement got her attention as well. She literally started from scratch. Contacting the county health department, gathering community support, and beginning with a small room in her school, Chan targeted this innovative plan toward students and parents in the community who needed these services the most.

Chan led the charge to convert her school of 100 percent minority and free/reduced-price lunch–eligible students from a school with the worst scores in the district to a high-performing charter school that was recognized as high-achieving and safe for students.

The move to charter status was a new challenge. Chan became even more involved in "managerial minutiae," such as elevator maintenance and other building items. "I even had to determine how many pots and pans to order," recounts Chan. Her efforts were covered by news media. "I was on *Good Morning America,* interviewed by Diane Sawyer," she recalls. "Our school was the first to declare charter status and claim independence [from the Los Angeles Unified School District] in order to get more accountability and results. But our scores had been at the bottom. We could not get worse. We had to change. Again, this consistent poor performance was a crisis that propelled us to change. We went from crack house to schoolhouse."

Chan credits dealing with crises with giving her the initiative to make important transformations: "A crisis allows you to take initiative and capture the knowledge, the skills, the attitude, and the human capital to create something new that helps solve persistent problems. All you need is persistence and confidence."

Address Behavioral Issues

It may be the kindergarten student who runs out of class without a moment's notice and without apparent reason. For the high school English Department head, it might be realizing that three papers are plagiarized—by top seniors accepted to prestigious universities. As school leaders, so much of our time is filled with managing these surprises, from both the student side and the adult side. These situations require action, and stakeholders are watching to see how we respond.

Chan says, "It's all about long-term relationships. I will find a way to connect with that student in preschool and find them anywhere in the community. Just like the Energizer bunny, I find a way to stay charged and keep the relationship strong." Relationships provide a long-lasting framework that goes a long way in helping leaders find relational, authentic ways to overcoming challenges that arise. If a parent, for instance, has heard about his child's academic success from the child's teacher, then he will be more likely to listen when the teacher calls about a behavioral issue or an ethical infraction.

Weather Budget Cuts

You find out at a principals' meeting that all high schools are losing between 3.0 and 7.0 Instructional FTE (full-time equivalent) positions. This cut is going to affect class size and scheduling and may force you to realign your instructional priorities. And you have just been making adequate yearly progress (AYP) by fractions of a percentage point. You have to deliver (and explain, and even defend) this bad news to your faculty at the next meeting. You have to sort out the "who" and the "how" in these cuts, and you know you will be the one who gets the irate calls and the looks of frustration in the hallway, and you know that the local newspaper will mention if your school does not meet the federal testing benchmarks.

Chan was once told that, due to a calendar change, she would lose more than $200,000. She responded by changing her school calendar to restore the funding. She laughs, "We even managed to add instructional days" as a result of these efforts. Although there is no quick and easy solution here, budget cuts can be weathered by reflecting on priorities and working as a team to ensure that all work effort and collaborative energies are focused on meeting those priorities. Aligning resources and efforts will serve the organization well even when the budget outlook eventually improves and priorities shift.

Cope with Staff Turnover

Even in the best of times, you will lose great people. The way you go about replacing them, from affirming their work and wishing them well to evaluating the right people to fill their roles, requires a variety of skill sets. There is often no formula for going about this set of tasks, which is why it is a challenge. "That principal is bleeding staff" is never a feel-good statement, yet turnover happens, often unrelated to a principal's actions. The key to overcoming this challenge is to ensure that your staff feels valued—sending personalized notes to all staff members will work wonders, as will giving them opportunities to be heard and to contribute—and to work, over time, to set a tone that values your colleagues. In addition, involving the grade- or subject-level team in which the new hire will serve in the hiring process builds a sense of shared investment and ownership.

Deal with Legal Issues

Getting a formal letter from an attorney starting with the words "Please be advised . . ." is never at the top of a principal's wish list. Yet working with the legal system will happen. Whether you're fielding calls from frustrated parents who want to sue you, dealing with law enforcement over a staff or student legal infraction, or working with social services to address parents' custody battles being squabbled over during a school function, these scenarios are always unique and multifaceted. Regardless of how rigorous our school-law course was, there is nothing like on-the-job experience to drive a leader to draw on his or her reasoning, reflection, and deliberation skills. As a school leader, you should familiarize yourself with relevant policy and legal statutes at the district, state, and federal levels and work closely with your legal liaison (often in human resources) when such situations arise. Keep in mind that not all threats to sue mature into action. Often, frustrated parties just want to be heard.

Action Items

As an educational leader, you are the one whom parents will want to hear from first, you are the one whom the media will want to quote, you are the one who will sign off on work orders to repair the damage, and you are the one who will answer to the superintendent. You are the one who wakes up each morning with the demands of the job in your mind. You are the one who bears the burden—and the privilege—of leading the school. You must be the one who takes the action.

Develop a Crisis Plan

When a crisis hits, you should have a well-thought-out plan that puts you and a trusted team into motion, regardless of the event. Although crisis plans are multifaceted and often incorporate a variety of scenarios, here are some components that every leader should consider when devising such a plan:

- **Composition of the team.** The crisis team should involve people whose work is embedded throughout the school community. In a school setting, team members may include the physical education teacher, the guidance counselor, the school nurse, a department head, the custodian, the secretary, and the entire administrative team. This team will constantly have its finger on the pulse of the school community in terms of outreach and input.

- **Communication protocol.** Use an up-to-date, working phone tree for internal staff communication. When you need to get a message out to the larger school community quickly, especially in times of tragedy, I recommend using a web-based program that alerts families both by phone and by e-mail. You never want the news media to beat you to the punch. Be succinct, clear, and professional, and assure the recipients that appropriate details will follow but that you want to ensure they receive timely and accurate information as families and the school community work together. The principal should designate the protocol and make it clear that any questions or requests for comments be handled in a consistent manner through the administrative office. This protocol should determine how events are shared and by whom, and should also address who works with the media and how.

- **Coordination with division resources.** During a serious crisis like a staff or student death, I coordinated with our division to get counseling support, deal with media requests, provide updates, and forge a sense of solidarity. Leaders throughout the division had encountered similar tragedies in their roles and were willing to share their guidance.

- **Reflection.** After the crisis, convene as a team to review each step that was taken. This is an opportunity to affirm what went right, correct what didn't, and consider next steps.

Align the Organization

Chan likens organizational alignment to "balancing and aligning the four wheels of your car." To go the distance, the wheels must be aligned. Chan describes "four wheels that are equally important in leading a school":

- **Strategic management.** Focus first on student needs, and then deploy human capital to meet those needs. Everything a leader does—from recruitment, induction, and training of staff to professional development and ongoing reflection—should be aligned strategically to the needs of the students in the learning environment.

- **Curriculum alignment.** Instructional delivery, accountability measures, and use of technology for learning should also be aligned to the needs of students. At Vaughn School, this alignment is focused on Response to Intervention (RTI) and on reaching and differentiating learning for the school's 1,200-plus English learners.

- **School culture.** The "sense of trust and the expectation that we can solve problems and create something new enable us to build an internal accountability system," Chan observes. Encompassing everyone in the school community, from students and staff to parents, this culture drives continual self-review and in-depth reflection that "goes beyond NCLB [No Child Left Behind] and runs like a clock."

- **Community resources.** The fact that Vaughn's school-based health clinic is thriving is a testament to Chan's vision for the school. Chan reaches out to the unemployed and "connects the dots of all these agencies and support structures" to help kids. Chan encourages leaders to fight the practice of "everybody waiting for everyone else to do something."

Prioritize Personal Health

Stay fit. Go outside. We need to breathe fresh air, recharge our batteries, work out, and stay energized. Being frazzled, exasperated, and out of shape does not speak well of one's priorities, and the organization suffers as well. Your own priorities and mood are reflected back in the mirror of the school. I noticed, as a teacher and principal, that whenever I smiled at others, they generally smiled back. And when I was exuberant and enthusiastic (and perhaps, at times, obnoxious or silly), those around me usually joined in. We are a reflection of our school, and vice versa. We must take care of ourselves.

Find Success Partners

In the potentially isolating position of school leader, it is important to stay linked to others. As a principal, I needed to work with colleagues to stay professionally recharged. Chan notes, "I never felt lonely in my work. I would talk to anyone I could about instruction. I would talk to my custodian. I now connect with other charter school principals. I find ways to talk about instructional strategies and various issues with trusted people I can bounce issues off of. And I talk with the kids. We need to hear from them and sit down and have an in-depth conversation with them. They will give us ideas as well!" Each leader should identify at least one success partner and capitalize on "the power of two" (Sterrett & Haas, 2009) to set goals, share instructional leadership strategies, encourage each other, and help each other grow as leaders.

Learn to Triage

When I was a principal, I was often asked, "How are you able to get it all done? How do you pick your battles?" The truth is, you simply cannot attend to every pressing issue at the same time. As Alex Carter noted, this job can kill you if you let it. You have to prioritize.

Here's an exercise in priorities. Imagine yourself as a single administrator in a middle school. The following things happen simultaneously:

- The fire marshal arrives, unannounced, for a periodic inspection, and, as principal, you must walk through the building with him to verify your school's adherence to code.
- The phone begins to ring; an irate parent who has refused to speak with you about a pressing issue has finally called you back.
- Your office associate notifies you that an upset 6th grader has again run into the woods. You are typically the only one he will respond to during this stage of flight.
- Three excited 7th graders have lugged in their ribbon-adorned project board to show you and are chatting loudly outside your office.

Four pressing issues at one moment: a not-uncommon situation for today's leaders. You need to consider three factors. In education, we love acronyms, so here goes: TIP.

1. First, in terms of **time**, what are the immediate repercussions that will result from your choice of action? Can some of these issues wait or be postponed without significant consequence?

2. Second, what is the **impact** on the "big picture," or greater school community? How will your decision to act affect the school and those in the school?

3. Third, which **people** (staff, volunteers, etc.) are available to help?

These three considerations guide me to look through a trifocal lens (see Figure 9.1) in picking my battle (see Figure 9.2).

Figure 9.1 | Trifocal TIP Response Perspective of Crisis Management

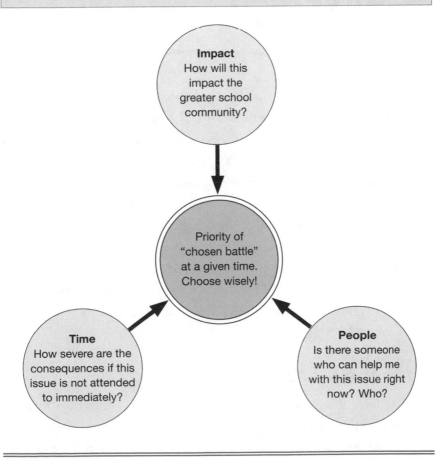

Figure 9.2 | **Sample TIP Response Chart**

Issue	Time	Impact	People	Total Score
The fire marshal needs you to walk with him through the building for an unannounced inspection.	2	1	2	5
An irate parent returns your call after refusing to speak with you earlier.	2	1	3	6
An upset 6th grader has run into the woods.	3	2	3	8
Excited 7th graders are waiting to show you their project board display.	2	1	3	6

Rankings key: 1= low priority; 2 = medium priority; 3 = high priority

As you can see, the upset student in the woods must take my attention. Safety comes first, and despite the fact that he has done this before, he cannot be left alone and is unlikely to respond to anyone but me. I really want to celebrate the students' project board, but I want my congratulations to be authentic and sincere, and I cannot give them my undivided attention until I resolve the first crisis. Similarly, I have tried calling the irate parent already; she can wait for my return call. And although I love the fire marshal, he will surely understand priority of crisis and either reschedule the inspection or speak to our custodian. I obviously do not sit down and complete a chart, but looking through the TIP lenses has helped me make quick-as-a-blink decisions in similar scenarios many times. And all the situations eventually do get resolved.

"I Am the Message"

Chan believes that school leaders must own results rather than look for excuses or others to blame. She is both motivator and connector. She has experienced tragedy, and will continue to do so as a building leader, yet she overcomes obstacles to bolster the collective efforts of the school community. By aligning the resources and harnessing the energy within and around the school community, she is able to translate challenges and crises into successes and solutions that benefit the students who need help the most. She does not simply speak for her school; she lives out this work daily: "I am not the messenger, I am the message."

She realizes that the role of the principal is to overcome challenges by translating what *should* be done into what *gets* done. By turning insights into action, she has realized enormous success for herself as a professional, for her community, and for each student who, in turn, beats the odds.

In-the-Field Activities

1. Identify a veteran leader, in a position similar to yours, whom you admire. Ask the leader about a crisis he or she experienced and his or her thoughts on the following components of crisis response:
   a. Readiness and response.
   b. Communication.
   c. Action and outcome.
   d. Reflection and next steps.

2. Pick several issues, tough scenarios, or crises that have occurred during the last year. What if they overlapped and you had to quickly prioritize a course of action? Look at Figures 9.1 and 9.2 and structure a TIP response.

3. While getting your yearly physical, your doctor informs you that your blood pressure is dangerously high and that you are 20 pounds overweight. This is the first time you have not gotten the "fit as a fiddle" diagnosis, and you realize that you need to make changes. What considerations, both professionally and personally, will you weigh as you determine next steps?

4. Review the Action Items from this chapter and develop a plan to implement at least one in your school setting. Consider the various challenges you have faced, and reflect on two of them. What might you do to "grow through" these crises and propel your school forward? Take stock of your crisis plan. Do you have the right people in place? Is your communication protocol ready? Review Chan's approach to organizational alignment. How would you describe your approach in these four areas? Finally, identify a success partner, if you have not already. Set aside a monthly time to meet for an hour and devise a format to collaborate on instructional leadership, accountability, and professional growth.

Conclusion

A scene from one of my favorite movies, *Indiana Jones and the Last Crusade*, often flashes through my mind when I am feeling crushed by on-the-job pressures. In this scene, the action hero and educator arrives from an incredible adventure in the seas off the Portuguese coast in 1938. Having survived beatings, snakes, a burning ship, betrayal, treachery, and the loss of a valuable artifact with his customary nonchalance, Professor Jones concludes a lecture on archaeology with his class. Overwhelmed by the hordes of students clamoring for his attention, the harried educator escapes the demands of his job by crawling out through his open office window. And he doesn't look back. *On to the next adventure.*

For today's teacher leaders and principals, that window escape can seem pretty appealing as we look at the piles of papers on our desk, the blinking office phone, and the unanswered e-mails. Yet we shoulder our burdens, knowing that we are up to the task. Although we may struggle and continually be reminded of our limitations in this role that would challenge Superman or Indiana Jones, we are the best fit for the job not only because of our experience and qualifications but also because of our unique insight in realizing what is important. It's important that we reach the student who comes to school hungry on Monday morning and the colleague who is facing personal problems while stressing out over the upcoming high-stakes tests. It's important that we decide how to reach the most rational and student-centered decision on how to reconcile a 10 percent cut to our already reduced budget. And it's important that we continue to bolster our school community by living a vision that is centered on all members of the school community growing and succeeding in a just manner.

In the end, we know that we do not have all the answers. It is essential that we lean on peers whom we admire, trust, and can learn from. We must work in an environment where we can respectfully ask questions and challenge long-held assumptions, looking at an issue from multiple angles and through different lenses. We must read. We must get outdoors and breathe. We must learn from one another and from those in the field who have faced similar challenges and pushed similar boulders up similar mountains. Our work is often one "tough case scenario" after another, in which there are no easy answers. But by relying on our wisdom and expertise, conferring with those we work with and for, and listening to and reflecting on voices in the field, we can translate insights into action that yields powerful results for our students—*all* students. This is important work. And we are ready. *On to the next adventure.*

Bibliography

Acheson, K. A., & Gall, M. D. (1992). *Techniques in the clinical supervision of teachers* (3rd ed.). White Plains, NY: Longman Publishing Group.

Barros, R. M., Silver, E. J., & Stein, R. E. K. (2009). School recess and group classroom behavior. *Pediatrics, 123*(2), 431–436.

Blair, D. (2009). The child in the garden: An evaluative review of the benefits of school gardening. *Journal of Environmental Education, 40*(2), 15–38.

Bolman, L. B., & Deal, T. E. (2003). *Reframing organizations: Artistry, choice, and leadership.* San Francisco: Jossey-Bass.

Bossidy, L., & Charan, R. (2002). *Execution: The discipline of getting things done.* New York: Crown Publishing.

Brooks-Young, S. (2009). *Making technology standards work for you: A guide to the NETS-A for school administrators with self-assessment activities* (2nd ed.). Washington, DC: International Society for Technology in Education.

Charles, C., & Louv, R. (2009, September). *Children's nature deficit: What we know—and don't know.* Santa Fe, NM: Children and Nature Network. Available: www.children andnature.org/downloads/CNNEvidenceoftheDeficit.pdf

Charles, C., Louv, R., & St. Antoine, S. (2010, October). *Children and Nature Network 2010 report.* Santa Fe, NM: Children and Nature Network. Available: www.children andnature.org/downloads/C&NNReport_2010.pdf

Charles, C., & Senauer, A. (2010). *Children's contact with the outdoors and nature: A focus on educators and educational settings.* Santa Fe, NM: Children and Nature Network. Available: www.childrenandnature.org/downloads/Educationsynthesis.pdf

Charney, R. (2002). *Teaching children to care: Classroom management for ethical and academic growth.* Turners Fall, MA: Northeast Foundation for Children.

Chenoweth, K. (2010). Leaving nothing to chance. *Educational Leadership, 68*(3), 16–21.

Christenbury, L. (2010). The flexible teacher. *Educational Leadership, 68*(4), 46–50.

Cibulka, J. G. (2009). Declining support for higher-education leadership preparation programs: An analysis. *Peabody Journal of Education, 84*(3), 453–466.

Collins, J. (2001). *Good to great.* New York: HarperCollins.

Connolly, M. (2007). Harried principals aren't helpful principals. *Principal, 86*(5), 32.

Cotton, K. (2003). *Principals and student achievement.* Alexandria, VA: ASCD.

Cuban, L. (2007). Hugging the middle: Teaching in an era of testing and accountability. *Education Policy Analysis Archives, 15*(1), 1–29.

Davies, B., & Brighouse, T. (2010). Passionate leadership. *Management in Education, 24*(4), 4–6.

Davies, P. (2010). On school educational technology leadership. *Management in Education, 24*(2), 55–61.

De Greene, K. B. (1982). *The adaptive organization: Anticipation and management of crisis.* New York: John Wiley & Sons.

Delpit, L. (2006). Lessons from teachers. *Journal of Teacher Education, 57*(3), 220–231.

Devaney, L. (2010, January 26). Our 10th annual tech-savvy superintendent awards. *ESchool News.* Available: www.eschoolnews.com/2010/01/26/our-10th-annual-tech-savvy-superintendent-awards/3/

DuFour, R. (2002). The learning-centered principal. *Educational Leadership, 59*(8), 12–15.

DuFour, R. (2004). What is a "professional learning community"? *Educational Leadership, 61*(8), 6–11.

Duke, D. L. (2010). *Differentiating school leadership.* Thousand Oaks, CA: Corwin Press.

Essex County Vocational Technical Schools. (2011). Mighty Newark Tech. Available: www.essextech.org/nt/nt_index.php

Fisher, D., & Frey, N. (2007). *Checking for understanding: Formative assessment techniques for your classroom.* Alexandria, VA: ASCD.

Four Winds Nature Institute. (2011). *Schoolyard habitat mini-grants.* Available: www.fwni.org/59.html

Fullan, M. (2001). *Leading in a culture of change.* San Francisco: Jossey-Bass.

Gallwey, W. T. (2000). *The inner game of work: Focus, learning, pleasure, and mobility in the workplace.* New York: Random House.

Gardner, H. (1999). *Intelligence reframed: Multiple intelligences for the 21st century.* New York: BasicBooks.

Gibbs, J. (2007, April 24). Outdoor classroom. *Las Cruces* (NM) *Sun-News.*

Goldring, E., & Schuermann, P. (2009). The changing context of K–12 education administration: Consequences for Ed.D. program design and delivery. *Peabody Journal of Education, 84*(1), 9–43.

Grandin, T. (1995). *Thinking in pictures: And other reports from my life with autism.* New York: Random House.

Hess, F. M. (2008). The new stupid. *Educational Leadership, 66*(4), 12–17.

Johnson, J. (2008). The principal's priority 1. *Educational Leadership, 66*(1), 72–76.

Kafele, B. (2010). Biographical information. Available: www.principalkafele.com/biography

Kafka, J. (2009). The principalship in historical perspective. *Peabody Journal of Education, 84*(3), 318–330.

Kise, J. A. G., & Russell, B. (2008). *Differentiated leadership: Effective collaboration, communication, and change through personality type.* Thousand Oaks, CA: Corwin Press.

Kriete, R. (2002). *The morning meeting book.* Greenfield, MA: Northeast Foundation for Children.

Kuo, F. E., & Faber Taylor, A. (2005). Kuo and Faber Taylor respond. *American Journal of Public Health, 95*(3), 371–372.

Lencioni, P. (2004). *Death by meeting: A leadership fable about solving the most painful problem in business.* San Francisco: Jossey-Bass.

Lester, S., & Maudsley, M. (2006, August 2). *Play, naturally: A review of children's natural play.* Commissioned for Playday 2006 by the Children's Play Council. Available: www.playday.org.uk/PDF/play-naturally-a-review-of-childrens-natural%20play.pdf

Louv, R. (2008). *Last child in the woods: Saving our children from nature-deficit disorder.* Chapel Hill, NC: Algonquin Books.

Louv, R. (2009). Do our kids have nature-deficit disorder? *Educational Leadership, 67*(4), 24.

Marzano, R. J. (2007). *The art and science of teaching: A comprehensive framework for effective instruction.* Alexandria, VA: ASCD.

Milken Family Foundation. (2010). Educator profile: Baruti Kafele. Retrieved August 6, 2010, from www.mff.org

Moran, P. (2010a). Twitter post. Retrieved August 18, 2010, from http://twitter.com/pammoran

Moran, P. (2010b, July 30). Staying relevant as a leader and learner [Blog post]. *Edurati Review.* Available: http://eduratireview.com/2010/07/leading-through-relevant-uncertainty

November, A. (2010). *Empowering students with technology* (2nd ed.). Thousand Oaks, CA: Corwin Press.

Ogden, C. L., Carroll, M. D., Curtin, L. R., Lamb, M. M., & Flegal, K. M. (2010). Prevalence of high body mass index in U.S. children and adolescents, 2007–2008. *The Journal of the American Medical Association, 303*(3), 242–249.

Palestini, R. H. (2003). *The human touch in educational leadership.* Lanham, MD: Scarecrow Press.

Patterson, K., Grenny, J., Maxfield, D., McMillan, R., & Switzler, A. (2008). *Influencer: The power to change anything.* New York: McGraw-Hill.

Payton, J., Weissberg, R. P., Durlak, J. A., Dymnicki, A. B., Taylor, R. D., Schellinger, K. B., et al. (2008). *The positive impact of social and emotional learning for kindergarten to eighth-grade students: Findings from three scientific reviews.* Chicago: Collaborative for Academic, Social, and Emotional Learning.

Popham, J. (2008). *Transformative assessment.* Alexandria, VA: ASCD.

Popham, J. (2010). *Homage to a hyphen: How to keep the formative-assessment process what it should be.* Prepared remarks as pre-conference reading for a June 20, 2011, Kentucky Leadership Networks Summer 2011 Administrators Conference, Lexington, KY, and for a February 9–10, 2011, meeting of the Council of Chief State School Officers Formative Assessment for Students and Teachers SCASS, Atlanta, GA.

Reeves, D. (2008). *Reframing teacher leadership to improve your school.* Alexandria, VA: ASCD.

Reeves, D. (2009). *Leading change in your school.* Alexandria, VA: ASCD.

Rivkin, M. (1997). The schoolyard habitat movement: What it is and why children need it. *Early Childhood Education Journal, 25*(1). Available: www.nwf.org/schoolyard/movement.cfm

Roller, W. (2009, February 27). Outdoor classroom helps inspire students, Gila teacher says. (Yuma, AZ) *The Sun.*

Schlechty, P. C. (2002). *Working on the work: An action plan for teachers, principals, and superintendents.* San Francisco: Jossey-Bass.

Schmoker, M. (1999). *Results: The key to continuous school improvement* (2nd ed.). Alexandria, VA: ASCD.

Shipps, D., & Kafka, J. (2009). Introduction to the special issue on the new politics of educational leadership. *Peabody Journal of Education, 84*(3), 279–282.

Socol, I. D. (2010). *Human communication* [Blog post]. Available: http://speedchange.blogspot.com/2010/05/human-communication.html

Sparks, D. (2007). What it means to be an outside-the-box leader. In P. D. Houston, A. M. Blankstein, & R. W. Cole (Eds.), *Outside the box leadership* (pp. 11–29). Thousand Oaks, CA: Corwin Press.

Sterrett, W. (2008). A principal looks at thirty. *Principal, 87*(5), 64.

Sterrett, W., & Fiddner, P. (2007). Snapshot portraits of math achievement: The vital role of math exit slips in the elementary setting. *Virginia Educational Leadership, 5*(1), 94–97.

Sterrett, W., & Haas, M. (2009). The power of two. *Educational Leadership, 67*(2), 78–80.

Sterrett, W., & JohnBull, R. (2009). Empowering misbehaving students: An effective schoolwide discipline plan must consistently support learning and instruction. *Principal, 88*(4). Available: www.naesp.org/resources/2/Principal/2009/M-Aweb3.pdf

Sterrett, W., Murray, B., & Sclater, K. (2011). Preemptive relationships: Teacher leadership in strengthening a school community. *Virginia Educational Leadership, 8*(1), 17–26.

Sterrett, W., Williams, B., & Catlett, J. (2010). Using technology and teamwork to enhance peer observations. *Virginia Educational Leadership, 7*(1), 65–71.

Tomlinson, C. A. (1999). *The differentiated classroom: Responding to the needs of all learners.* Alexandria, VA: ASCD.

Tomlinson, C. A., & McTighe, J. (2006). *Integrating differentiated instruction and Understanding by Design.* Alexandria, VA: ASCD.

U.S. Department of Education, Office of Planning, Evaluation and Policy Development, Policy and Program Studies Service. (2007). *State and local implementation of the No Child Left Behind Act, Volume III—Accountability under NCLB: Interim report.* Washington, DC: Author. Available: www2.ed.gov/rschstat/eval/disadv/nclb-accountability/nclb-accountability.pdf

Wagner, T., & Kegan, R. (2006). *Change leadership: A practical guide to transforming our schools.* San Francisco: Jossey-Bass.

Wei, R. C., Darling-Hammond, L., & Adamson, F. (2010). *Professional development in the United States: Trends and challenges.* Dallas, TX: National Staff Development Council.

Weilbacher, M. (2009). The window into green. *Educational Leadership, 66*(8), 38.

Wiliam, D. (2007). Changing classroom practice. *Educational Leadership, 65*(4), 36.

Index

Information in figures is indicated by *f*.

About the Author

 William Sterrett serves on the faculty of the Watson School of Education at the University of North Carolina at Wilmington. A former principal and teacher, Sterrett earned his B.S. at Asbury University in Wilmore, Kentucky, and his Ph.D. at the University of Virginia. Named a 2008 Milken National Educator as principal, Sterrett was recognized in 2009 by the Virginia General Assembly for his work. Sterrett resides in Wilmington, North Carolina, with his wife, Stephanie, and their three sons. He may be reached at the Watson School of Education, The University of North Carolina at Wilmington, 601 South College Road, Wilmington, NC 28403-5980; sterrettw@uncw.edu. He may be followed on Twitter via @billsterrett.